RECONSTRUCT

THE INTERNAL BARRIERS
THAT KEEP YOUR GENIUS FROM LEADING

Princess-Anne Emeka-Obiajunwa

Cover design and Book layout:
colourplaygraphics@gmail.com

Publisher:
suttonandbriggs@outlook.com

DEDICATION

To you, my reader, may you excel in your sphere

CONTENTS

INTRODUCTION

Leadership is not solely determined by competence or aspiration; it is also constrained or expanded by one's internalized beliefs about what they are permitted to become.

Many women enter leadership spaces as capable, experienced, and prepared individuals, yet find that leadership roles do not open in the way they expected. Women meet expectations, handle responsibility, and deliver results, but influence seems conditional, and progress feels slower than it should.

Most individuals attribute the problem to external factors such as the environment, opportunity, timing, or team, without recognizing the internal constraints that may be shaping their outcomes. Others turn inward, questioning their confidence, readiness, or boldness. What is rarely examined, however, is that leadership experiences are often limited by what a leader perceives as permissible within their own mind.

For many women, internal scripts shape how much responsibility feels justified, how much visibility feels permitted, and how much authority feels legitimate. These scripts do not eliminate capability, but they strongly influence leadership behaviour and, as a result, affect access, opportunity, and influence.

This book is written for women who are already capable but sense that something internal interferes with how they respond to visibility, influence, and authority. It offers clarity about the internal patterns that shape leadership behaviour and shows how those patterns can be intentionally revised.

You will see how fear, guilt, shyness, and insecurity influence leadership from within, and how specific correctives can remove the internal barriers that have limited your leadership expression.

By the end of this book, you will have practical tools to lead from alignment rather than effort, and from stability instead of pressure.

PART ONE

LEADERSHIP POSTURE

How did my leadership posture form?

CHAPTER ONE

TRACE YOUR LEADERSHIP ORIGIN

My earliest understanding of leadership came from home. I grew up as the firstborn daughter (Ada) in a Nigerian family, and that position created its own rhythm long before I knew the word leadership.

I had one younger sister for many years before other siblings arrived, so most of my early life was framed around the two of us. Being the "Ada" came with its own script. It meant responsibility, maturity, and sacrifice. It meant attending to someone else before thinking of myself. It meant stepping into a role simply because that was what firstborn daughters did. This foundational *"Ada duty"* became the springboard for my leadership identity work, reshaping early responsibility into conscious leadership practice that supports the identity shifts explored in this book.

For me, leadership began as service to my younger sister. Not purposeful service. Not reflective service. Not even conscious service. It was simply what I learned to do. I carried bags, solved conflicts, answered questions, and completed the tasks expected of the older child. I did not recognize it as influence; I understood it as duty.

As I grew older, I began to wonder what leadership looked like for someone who was not firstborn. How is leadership shaped in a second child without those early responsibilities? How does it form in a third child, or a fourth? What is leadership for a girl who never had a younger sibling to guide? What does leadership look like for the child who never had to protect, mediate, or sacrifice?

Even within the same home, each child forms a different relationship with responsibility, influence, and expectation.

These early contrasts matter because they shape leadership identity long before we understand the meaning of the word.

My younger sister's leadership formation contrasted with mine from the start. While I carried the weight of chores and supported her, she had fewer household responsibilities and greater freedom to choose her activities and interests. I followed a structured routine shaped by duty, but she had space to observe, experiment, and pursue what intrigued her.Outside the home, leadership took on a different meaning. In school, leadership was tied to visibility. It involved standing in front of others and holding a role that people recognized. That was why I aspired to be class captain, leadership had become visible, and with it came recognition.

I was not given the position in primary school, yet I influenced people. Friends looked up to me. Classmates involved me. Only then did I realize that even without a title, I had influence. I simply did not have an official role.

By my second term in secondary school, I became the class captain, a recognition that came not from campaigning but from the way I handled responsibility. I organized class tasks, mediated disagreements, supported my peers, and carried myself with a sense of stability that teachers could trust. Eventually, I became the Senior Prefect Girl.

At the time, my school did not have a Senior

Prefect Girl position. There was a Senior Prefect Boy, a Deputy Senior Prefect Boy, and a Deputy Senior Prefect Girl. The assumption was that the highest leadership role belonged to boys. Girls could support. We could assist. We could participate but not lead the entire student body.

Your competence could become the reason an organization evolves.

When it got to my turn, the school created a new position, Senior Prefect Girl. I believe the school did this because they knew the value of my contribution to the school would be limited without the right leadership structure.

That experience taught me something more important than anything I learnt in that season of my life. I learnt that a woman's competence could become the reason an organization evolves. When women lead, structures evolve. Assumptions are challenged. New possibilities emerge. This is why women's leadership matters.

No Fixed Route to Leadership

What about the woman who was not a senior prefect or a first born like me?

Research shows that leadership does not emerge from a single path. Longitudinal and developmental studies demonstrate that early leadership foundations are shaped through diverse experiences, including family responsibilities, creative expression, independence, and formative social roles.[1,2] This variation confirms that leadership identities can originate from many contexts rather than a fixed developmental route.

You may not have been the firstborn. You may not have been giving major responsibilities at an early age. You may never have borne a title, formal role, or any recognized leadership position. You may even be reading this and thinking, "But I was never chosen. I was never seen. I was never invited into leadership." If that feels true for you, I want you to hear this clearly, leadership begins wherever influence finds you.

Consider Sarah

Sarah Plummet (Not actual name), never held a title in school, never led a team, and was not chosen for anything that looked like leadership. She grew up believing she was simply the quiet one in the background. Yet whenever her family faced tension, she was the one who calmed the room. When conflicts arose among friends, people instinctively came to her to help them make sense of what happened.

At work, colleagues often waited for her assessment before making decisions, not that she had any leadership position but because her perspective brought clarity.

The diversity in leadership origin demonstrates that there is no single path to developing leadership skills.

For years, Sarah dismissed these patterns as personality traits. She did not see them as leadership. It was only later, when a manager pointed out that the team relied on her judgment, that she recognised what had been happening all along. Influence had been present in her life long before any formal role appeared. Leadership did not arrive with a title. It showed itself in the way others relied on her for clarity.

Sarah's story demonstrates that leadership does not begin with recognition. It begins with influence, even when the leader does not yet see it as leadership.

For some women, leadership started with caring for siblings. For others, it began in moments of survival, difficulty, or unexpected responsibility. Some discovered leadership through creativity, problem-solving, resilience, or the ability to make things work when circumstances demanded it. Many learned to lead without ever being acknowledged for it. This diversity in leadership origins shows that there is no single path to developing leadership skills.

Leadership is often evident in actions and influence long before it is recognized formally. Titles do not validate leadership. Your leadership origin is not less; it is simply different. And as you continue reading, you will see why your path, your patterns, and your beginnings are just as legitimate, powerful, and worthy of recognition as any other.

When Early Leadership Definitions No Longer Fit

Leadership feels misaligned for many women because the definition they inherited as girls no longer fits the women they have become.

Early lessons about leadership tend to follow women into adulthood, shaping their instincts long after the environment has changed.[3.] Some women were taught that leadership means sacrifice without rest. Some learned that leadership belongs to men and that their contribution is to support, not direct. Others learned that leadership requires a boldness they were forbidden to display. Some were praised for being quiet, so visibility now feels unsafe. Others like me were trained to be responsible from childhood, so pulling back feels like irresponsibility.

These internalized expectations create pressure that appears as burnout from doing too much, missed opportunities from staying silent, and hesitation rooted in early lessons that discouraged assertiveness. A woman's career can slow down when she avoids roles that feel misaligned with the identity she was conditioned to uphold.

Internalized lessons influence how women engage with leadership opportunities, either constraining expression or enabling it.

The following example is a composite case based on patterns I observe in coaching practice. Let's call her "Amisha (not her real name).

Amisha, brilliant by every standard, was overlooked for a promotion she fully deserved. She had the competence, the results, and the credibility, but she continued to work quietly in the background without advocating for herself. This was not because she lacked ambition. It was something from her childhood years.

Growing up, Amisha was praised for being the quiet, compliant child, so speaking up felt unnatural as she wanted to stay compliant. This internalised expectation cost her an opportunity she had earned.

I have also seen the opposite happen to Amisha when she examined the early lessons that shaped her. With coaching, intentional reflection, and the courage to challenge old expectations, she redefined her leadership identity. Amisha embraced visibility, took responsibility for difficult decisions, and eventually led her team through a defining project that earned her a promotion she once believed was unreachable.

Amisha's journey shows that early scripts can be unlearned and replaced with healthier ones that support your purpose.

The leadership struggles women face today are rarely about ability; they are rooted in inherited expectations and early definitions shaped by childhood roles, cultural expectations, family dynamics, and the environments where leadership was first observed, encouraged or denied.

Like Amisha, the leadership struggles women face today are rarely about ability; they are rooted in inherited expectations and early definitions shaped by childhood roles, cultural expectations, family dynamics, and the environments where leadership was first observed, encouraged or denied.

LEADERSHIP ORIGIN EXERCISE
(Five Minutes)

Recall your earliest memory of leadership.

Did it begin through action, observation, responsibility, or comparison?

Notice the first emotion attached to that memory. Was it strength, pressure, silence, pride, or obligation?

Consider the environment around that moment. Did leadership come to you as duty, expectation, opportunity, or circumstance?

Write down whatever stands out most clearly. A picture. A feeling. A sentence. A role. A moment.

Finally, identify how that early definition still shows up in your life today. What parts of it support you? What parts of it hold you back?

WHAT TO DO WITH WHAT YOU DISCOVER

What you uncovered in the leadership origin exercise is not a verdict on your story. It is information. It shows you where your leadership identity began, and it gives you language for patterns you may have carried through the years. Here is how to steward the information you now have about your leadership origin:

Acknowledge What Strengthened You

You may notice early qualities that still serve you today, qualities like responsibility, empathy, initiative, adaptability, or resilience. These are indicators of your leadership capacity.

Notice The Emotions That Influence Your Behaviour

You may also uncover patterns that made leadership feel complicated. Patterns such as silence, caution, over-carrying, shrinking, or self-monitoring. Do not judge them. They were formed in environments where you were learning to survive, belong, or succeed. These patterns are not your identity; they are simply old strategies that once served a purpose.

Write down your discoveries

You are not required to change anything yet. At this stage, your only task is to be aware.

Decide

Ask yourself, "What do I want to keep, and what is that belief that no longer supports who I am becoming?" This question prepares your heart and mind for the internal reconstruction work ahead.

WHAT TO REMEMBER

- Leadership is shaped by early roles, responsibilities, and what was rewarded or ignored.
- Every woman's leadership origin is valid, whether rooted in duty, survival, creativity, silence, or independence.
- Leadership does not begin with a title; it begins with influence.
- Growth requires recognising and releasing the beliefs that no longer serves the leader you are becoming.

CHAPTER TWO

UNDERSTAND YOUR LEADERSHIP BEHAVIOUR

Leadership behavior refers to the observable actions through which leaders enact their roles and influence outcomes. The behavior includes decision-making, communication, pressure management, and responsibility handling, and are shaped by internal processes rather than skill alone.[123]

Leaders act from an internal structure made up of their beliefs, emotional tendencies, self-regulation patterns and behavioural instincts.[4]

This chapter examines the internal structure using the *Internal Leadership Posture Model.*

The Internal Leadership Posture Model

The Internal Leadership Posture Model (ILPM) articulates the developmental pathway through which early emotional roots give rise to an Inner Script, how that script consolidates into an Internal Leadership Posture (ILP), and how that posture governs observable leadership behaviour.

As illustrated in the model, emotional roots form the foundational layer of leadership development. These roots organise meaning and belief at the level of the Inner Script. Over time, the Inner Script stabilises into a consistent internal leadership posture, which then expresses itself outwardly as leadership behaviour.

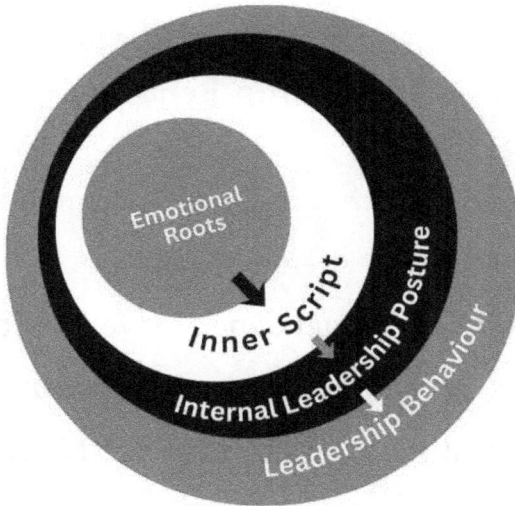

The Internal Leadership Posture
RECONSTRUCT : The Internal Barriers That Keep Your Genius From Leading
(SheLeadership Advantage™ Book 1)
© 2026 PRINCESS-ANNE EMEKA-OBIAJUNWA

The Internal Leadership Posture Model (ILPM) posits that leadership behaviour is not primarily the product of skill or context alone, but the outcome of a layered internal process shaped long before formal leadership responsibility begins. Understanding this internal process enable leaders interpret their leadership behaviour.

The Emotional Roots of Leadership Behaviour

Leadership research recognizes that emotion plays a significant role in leadership behaviour.[5]
Different emotional tendencies give rise to distinct leadership responses, particularly under pressure. The Internal Leadership Posture Model (ILPM) examines four core emotional roots (fear, guilt, insecurity, and shyness) to explain how these tendencies shape leadership behavior. Each root is anchored in evidence from leadership and emotion research.

Fear

Fear diminishes visibility, promotes avoidance behaviors, and leads to more cautious or withdrawn leadership responses. Research on fear-based leadership shows that leaders who experience heightened fear are more likely to retreat, minimize exposure, and act defensively in leadership situations.

The Internal Leadership Posture Model explains how emotional roots shape the Inner Script, how that script forms an Internal Leadership Posture, and how that posture produces leadership behavior.

Guilt

Guilt drives leaders over-responsibility, self-imposed pressure, and an internal drive to carry more than is sustainable. Studies show that guilt-prone individuals take on disproportionate responsibility for group outcomes and feel personally accountable for maintaining harmony and success.[7] These tendencies can strengthen or strain leadership depending on how they are managed.

Insecurity

Insecurity affects confidence, belonging and voice. Leadership research demonstrates that when leaders are insecure about their role, competence, or identity, they become defensive, hesitant, and more likely to protect themselves instead of leading objectively.[8] Job-insecurity studies also show that leaders respond to insecurity with anxiety-driven behaviors that distort decision-making.[9]

Shyness

Shyness reflects self-consciousness, fear of evaluation, and social inhibition, which often lead to reduced contribution even when the person has the capacity to deliver. In leadership research, these tendencies are represented by the personality dimension of extraversion.

The four emotional roots of leadership behavior are fear, Guilt, Insecurity, Shyness

Meta-analytic evidence shows that lower social boldness (low extraversion) significantly reduces leadership emergence and leadership expression.[9]

The Inner Script

The **Inner Script (IS)** is formed long before any conscious decision to lead. Inner script exists whether or not leadership was ever part of your plans. The inner script influences how leaders approach opportunities, relate to others, interpret feedback and respond to pressure[10].

The inner script teaches what is perceived as safe, what is perceived as risky, and what actions or inactions are required for belonging. Long before the term *leader* is used to describe oneself, this script is already shaping how responsibility is handled, how expression occurs, and how interaction unfolds within leadership contexts.[11,12] Research shows that women internalize relational expectations and behavioral norms early in life, and these internalized patterns influence how women later perceive themselves, interpret responsibility and engage with leadership opportunities.[13]

How the Inner Script is Formed

The Inner Script is formed through moments that influence your self-perception, your sense of safety, your relational instincts and the way you handle pressure.

Some women learned responsibility early, felt the emotional weight of duty, and were needed, depended on or praised for being dependable until responsibility became tied to worth. Over time, the emotion of pressure settled into an Inner Script that says, "I must carry this," forming an instinct to endure, persist and hold everything together.

Some women learned that acceptance depended on harmony and felt anxious at the thought of conflict. Conflict was associated with disapproval, while peace was associated with safety and acceptance. Heightened awareness of others' moods and reactions became an approach to safety.

Over time, this awareness settled into an Inner Script that says, "I must keep the peace," forming an instinct to mediate, please and stabilize an environment.

Other women learned that affection came through performance and felt insecure about being valued without achievement. Praise followed results, so productivity became the pathway to connection. Over time, insecurity settled into an Inner Script that says, "I am valued for what I produce," forming an instinct to strive, achieve and prove.

For many women, childhood was a blend of these emotional lessons. Families celebrated resilience but discouraged vulnerability. Others valued responsibility but overlooked emotional needs. Many environments taught girls to serve, support and accommodate long before they were encouraged to lead, speak or advocate, if they were encouraged at all.

THE INNER SCRIPT DIAGNOSTIC

Before you proceed, pause to assess which emotion has shaped your leadership instincts the most.

The Inner Script shows up differently in every woman, but most of us have one internal leadership posture that influences how we lead, respond and make decisions . The questions are designed to help you identify your dominant posture. Choose the statements that feel most true for you without overthinking. Your answers will reveal the emotional root influencing your inner script.

THE INNER SCRIPT
DIAGNOSTIC TOOL

For each of the seven categories, select the statement that best reflects your experience.

Which situation is most uncomfortable for you?

Being noticed or singled out (**Fear**)

Being expected to carry more than you can handle (**Guilt**)

Being evaluated or compared with others (**Insecurity**)

Being asked to speak before you feel prepared (**Shyness**)

Which belief most strongly drives your reactions?

"If people notice me, things might go wrong." (**Fear**)

"If I do not handle this, everything will fall apart." (**Guilt**)

"If I am not careful, I could lose my place."

(Insecurity)

"If I say the wrong thing, it will stay with me."
(Shyness)

How do you protect yourself emotionally?

I avoid drawing attention to myself. (Fear)

I feel compelled to step in even when others should handle it. **(Guilt)**

I change my tone or position to avoid tension. **(Insecurity)**

I delay speaking or acting until I feel completely certain. **(Shyness)**

When expectations suddenly increase, what is your first response?

I try to stay out of the spotlight. *(Fear)*

I take on additional responsibility without being asked. *(Guilt)*

I become highly attentive to how others may react.

(Insecurity)

I hesitate even when I have something important to contribute. *(Shyness)*

Which early message feels most familiar to your formative experience?

"Stop exposing yourself." **(Fear)**
"You are responsible for your siblings." **(Guilt)**
"You must not disappoint this family." **(Insecurity)**
"Be Quiet. Girls are to be seen, not heard." **(Shyness)**

Which adult pattern do you most recognise in your current leadership behaviour?

I withdraw or hesitate at critical moments. **(Fear)**
I consistently assume emotional or practical responsibility for others. **(Guilt)**
I frequently doubt my judgement despite adequate competence. **(Insecurity)**
I restrain or filter my contribution before speaking.

(Shyness)

Which aspect of leadership is most emotionally taxing for you?

Being seen and scrutinised. **(Fear)**
Being constantly depended upon. **(Guilt)**
Being judged or evaluated. **(Insecurity)**
Speaking openly in public or group spaces.
(Shyness)

Interpreting the Pattern

Your dominant posture is the category you selected the most. Your secondary posture is the next most frequent category. Most women carry a blend of these emotional roots, but one usually drives leaders' instinctive responses to responsibility, visibility, and pressure.

WHAT TO REMEMBER

- Leadership behaviour refers to how leaders act, respond, and make decisions in leadership situations.
- Leaders operate from an internal posture formed by beliefs, emotions, habits, and instinct.
- Emotional roots such as fear, guilt, or insecurity influence how leaders handle visibility, pressure, and evaluation.
- The Internal Leadership Posture Model shows how internal patterns shape external behaviour.

CHAPTER THREE

THE INTERNAL LEADERSHIP POSTURE

The internal leadership Posture is formed by the Inner Script. This posture becomes the instinct that shapes how leaders respond to responsibility, visibility and pressure, often long before they realize its influencing.

Early in life, girls absorb emotional expectations

such as compliance, caution, nurturance, guilt and self-restraint, and these internalized emotional norms shape how they behave in leadership contexts later.[1]

Research on women's leadership development shows that the emotional messages absorbed in girlhood become the patterns that shape how women interpret responsibility, and influence in adulthood.[2] Understanding these emotional roots makes it easier to see why leaders lead the way they do and why certain responses feel natural. The sections below examine how each emotional root develops into a distinct leadership posture in adulthood.

Fear-Rooted Leadership Posture

The fear-rooted posture develops in leaders whose Inner Script has established visibility as a condition associated with threat or adverse consequences. This posture forms within environments where visibility is linked to conflict, correction, or disappointment. As a protective adaptation, leaders learn to minimise exposure, exercise caution, and remain unobtrusive.

In leadership contexts, women with a fear-rooted posture may hesitate to step into visible leadership roles even when they possess the required competence. Leadership visibility is experienced as disruptive rather than enabling. Attention is interpreted as unsafe rather than strategic. Although leadership capacity remains intact, protective instinct governs behaviour.

Lived Experience

AMARA

From Southeastern Nigeria (Igbo)

Amara Igbokwe (Name Changed) grew up in a close knit Igbo family in Southeastern Nigeria, where restraint, respect, and emotional composure were strongly valued. She was praised as the compliant child, the one who did not argue, did not raise her voice, and did not disrupt the emotional order of the home. Calmness was considered a virtue and sustaining it became an unspoken expectation.

Women with a fear rooted posture may hesitate to move into leadership roles even when they possess the required competence.

Amara learned early that visibility unsettled the emotional balance the adults around her worked to maintain. A direct question, a firm opinion, or an expressed need drew attention she had learned to avoid. Over time, she internalized the belief that being noticeable was risky. As a result, she learned to move through her world with caution, controlled expression, and reduced exposure.

These emotional lessons extended beyond childhood. In school, she performed at a high academic level but remained quiet in class. Teachers recognized her competence but saw little of her emerging leadership potential. In adulthood, she became a reliable and highly capable colleague whose work was consistently strong but rarely visible. Her team trusted her, yet she was often overlooked for roles that required public presence or influence.

Leadership opportunities arose, yet she hesitated each time. The hesitation was not due to a lack of ability, but to the perceived cost of being seen.

Guilt-Driven Leadership Posture

The guilt driven posture develops in leaders who

learned early that responsibility was their primary role within the family or group system. They functioned as emotional stabilisers, managing tension, solving problems, and sustaining team dynamics. Over time, their Inner Script absorbed the implicit belief that personal worth is contingent upon usefulness to the group.

In leadership contexts, women with a guilt driven posture assume excessive responsibility. They experience difficulty resting, requesting support, or relinquishing control. Delegation is interpreted as imposing on others, and withdrawal is experienced as failure. Their competence remains high, yet it is accompanied by persistent internal pressure that drives overextension rather than sustainable leadership practice.

Lived Experience

PALOMA

From Bogotá, Colombia

Paloma Perez (Name Changed) grew up in Bogotá in a close multigenerational family where care responsibility was shared. As the eldest daughter, she naturally became the dependable one. She supported younger relatives and assisted her parents during demanding seasons. She became attuned to fatigue in others and moved quickly to ease it. Paloma sensed emotional tension and acted quickly to avert it. Over time, these patterns consolidated into an internal script that made her believe she was only as valuable as she supports others.

As an adult, Paloma is the colleague everyone trusts. She anticipates needs before they surface, remembers what others overlook, and intervenes without hesitation. Her competence is evident, and her calm presence brings order to complex situations.

Beneath this strength, however, is a persistent

difficulty with rest. Slowing down feels unfamiliar. Asking for help feels like an imposition. Delegation feels like transferring a burden she believes she should carry herself. When leadership opportunities emerge, Paloma accepts them, not out of a desire for visibility or authority, but from a deep internalised sense of obligation. Responsibility still feels like her primary identity.

Paloma's guilt driven leadership posture formed in a home where contribution, maturity, and reliability were deeply reinforced.

Women with a guilt driven leadership posture assume excessive responsibility. They experience difficulty resting, requesting support, or relinquishing control.

Over time, Paloma internalised the belief that her

worth was directly linked to how much she could do for others.

Insecurity Shaped Leadership Posture

Insecurity shaped leadership posture develops in leaders whose early relational environments linked acceptance to compliance. Such leaders learned to monitor social dynamics closely, anticipate expectations, and regulate their expression in order to preserve belonging. Over time, their Inner Script internalised the belief that acceptance must be earned rather than assumed.

In leadership contexts, women with insecurity shaped leadership posture demonstrate high relational sensitivity and emotional awareness, yet they hesitate to assert themselves when required. Such women moderate their tone, temper visibility, and prioritise relational stability. Conflict is experienced as threatening, and self-advocacy is seen as a risk.

Lived Experience

DEEPTI

From Kerala, India

Deepti Devi ((Name Changed)) grew up in Kerala in a family were success and family reputation mattered. Deepti's parents cared for her, and they were firm. Academic excellence was expected and affirmation was sparingly given .

Comparison was part of daily life. If Deepti did well, someone else had done better. If she got something right, it was simply what was expected. If she made a mistake, the response was swift because it was seen as reflecting on the whole family.

Over time, Deepti internalized an Inner Script that linked acceptance to perfection. As a child, this made her watch people closely. She learned to read moods, to anticipate reactions, and to adjust her behaviour accordingly. She replayed conversations in her mind, searching for what she might have said wrong. She learned to hide uncertainty and act composed, even when she felt unsure inside.

Women with Insecurity Shaped Leadership Posture demonstrate high relational sensitivity and emotional awareness, yet they hesitate to assert themselves when required.

As an adult, Deepti is intelligent, diligent, and highly capable. She delivers excellent work, but the excellence is driven by insecurity. She reads messages repeatedly before sending them. She rehearses her words before speaking in meetings.

She asks for feedback but braces herself for criticism.

Deepti finds it hard to trust colleagues, not because they are unkind, but because her Inner Script keeps warning her that she may be judged. When insecurity rises, she becomes guarded. She speaks less. She retreats from discussion. At times, her withdrawal is misunderstood as arrogance, when it is a form of defence

Leadership opportunities attract and unsettle her at the same time. She accepts them because they confirm her competence, but the visibility of leadership still makes her uneasy.

Deepti's insecurity shaped leadership posture formed in a home where excellence was expected, comparison was common, and being scrutinised was a norm. She learned to protect herself through constant self-monitoring and perfection. That early training still shapes how she leads today, contributing to a non-assertive leadership style.

Shyness Formed Leadership Posture

The shyness formed posture develops in leaders whose Inner Script was formed by social inhibition. Such leaders grew up in environments where speaking up was discouraged.

Leaders with this posture do not doubt their ideas, but they require extended internal readiness before voicing them. They reflect deeply, rehearse carefully, and often prefer accuracy over immediacy.

In leadership contexts, women with a shy internal leadership posture are thoughtful, perceptive, and strategically attentive although they hesitate to express themselves.

Lived Experience

CHARLOTTE

From Surrey, England

Charlotte Charles (Name Changed) grew up in Surrey in a warm but hands-off household. Her parents were gentle and easy going, the kind who believed that children should grow at their own pace. They rarely corrected her directly, and when she hesitated or struggled to articulate something, they stepped in and finished the sentence for her. When she felt uncomfortable, they changed the subject quickly rather than helping her deal with the discomfort. Nothing in her upbringing was harsh, but very little guided her toward finding her own voice.

Over time, keeping quiet became her default because it made interactions smooth and predictable. Adults praised her for being polite and well behaved. Teachers described her as easy going. Relatives referred to her shyness with affectionate approval, and this shaped her understanding of self. She was not discouraged from speaking, but she was never supported in navigating uncertainty, discomfort or the awkwardness of expression.

In school, Charlotte often knew the answer but held back until she was absolutely certain. She worried that she might explain the idea poorly or misunderstand the question, and the potential embarrassment felt worse than the reward of speaking.

The shyness formed Leadership posture develops in women whose Inner Script was formed by social inhibition. They grew up in environments where speaking up was discouraged.

During discussions, she stepped aside because she did not want to interrupt or risk getting lost in the pace. She watched confident and outspoken classmates receive attention.

As an adult, Charlotte is perceptive, reflective, and cognitively engaged. Charlotte processes information with considerable depth, often waiting for an ideal moment to contribute, a moment that rarely materialises.

Consequently, her quiet nature is misinterpreted as disengagement, when in fact it represents a long-standing strategy for managing the self-consciousness cultivated in childhood.

Leadership opportunities evoke a familiar internal tension for Charlotte. She worries about making mistakes in the presence of others or having her intentions misread. Although she prepares thoroughly, her caution tends to override her capability in critical moments.

Laying low once offered her psychological safety, and that early protective instinct now accompanies her into leadership contexts. Beneath her hesitation lies intelligence and leadership potential that her internal posture has not yet allowed to fully surface.

WHAT TO REMEMBER

- Inner Scripts become leadership posture.
- Internal Leadership posture shapes leadership behaviour.
- Fear, Guilt, Shyness and Insecurity shaped leadership postures are protective, not defective.

PART TWO

COST AND MECHANISMS

Why does this posture persist and what is it costing me?

CHAPTER FOUR

THE COST OF AN UNREVISED INTERNAL LEADERSHIP POSTURE

Strategies formed for protection in early contexts can become restrictive in leadership roles. When left unrevised, these strategies constrain leadership effectiveness rather than support it, with consequences that unfold across three interrelated domains.

Intrapersonal, shaping the internal world of the leader, including leadership capacity, emotional regulation, and psychological wellbeing.

Interpersonal, shaping how the leader is experienced by others, including perception, relationships, credibility, and influence.

Contextual, shaping how the leader operates within organizational and social environments, including access to opportunity and strategic contribution.

The cost to leadership capacity

When an internal leadership posture consolidates into a barrier, its effects extend beyond personal discomfort. The barrier directly constrains leadership capacity by limiting the range, confidence, and effectiveness with which leadership can be exercised.[1]

Leadership capacity is not limited to innate ability or talent. Leadership Capacity also includes what a leader can bear, steward, and sustain over time.[2]

A misaligned leadership posture progressively constrains this capacity by reducing the level of responsibility that can be carried without anxiety, the degree of authority that can be exercised without internal strain, and the depth of influence that can be enacted without self-doubt.[3]

An unrevised internal leadership posture produces loss across interpersonal, intrapersonal, Contextual domains.

When internal regulation is compromised, leadership effectiveness reduces even when competence remains.

The Cost to Mental Health

Misalignment between internal posture and the emotional and relational demands of leadership drives leaders to rely on compensatory patterns that deplete psychological resources faster than they can be restored.[4]

This makes Leaders apply excessive effort to offset insecurity, assume unsustainable responsibility as guilt reframes rest as negligence, and restrict engagement when fear interprets leadership demands as a threat. Over time, these patterns narrow emotional capacity and reduce relational engagement, because internal strain remains unrelieved.[5,6]

As this strain accumulates, its effects become difficult to ignore. Leaders experience persistent fatigue that rest does not resolve, growing resentment toward responsibilities once carried willingly, and a gradual decline in motivation.[2]

These responses reflect the psychological cost of prolonged self-regulation and internal overextension. Leaders withdraw from opportunities they once desired, not because purpose has been lost, but because the emotional cost of sustained engagement has become too high.[6] When left unaddressed, the consequence is not only reduced leadership effectiveness, but the progressive erosion of psychological well-being and sense of self.[2,6]

The Cost to reputation

Leadership is evaluated through visible behaviour, not intention. Internal leadership posture, therefore, matters because it shapes how leaders are interpreted. Leadership credibility is formed through observable behavioural signals, particularly under pressure, rather than through insight, motivation, or underlying capability.[7,8]

When internal posture is misaligned with the psychological and relational demands of leadership, leaders operate through emotional patterns that deplete energy faster than it can be restored.

When internal posture remains unexamined, emotional states translate into predictable behavioural cues. Fear may register as hesitation, guilt as over-availability, insecurity as excessive justification, and shyness as reduced contribution. These signals shape how leaders are perceived, regardless of their competence or judgment.[9,10]

When behavioural cues consistently contradict underlying capability, reputation becomes driven by appearance rather than capacity. Leadership credibility is therefore shaped by what others observe in action, not by what leaders intend. [7,8]

Sustained strategic contribution becomes difficult when internal resources are consumed by posture management instead of engagement with the work.

The Cost to Relationships and Influence

Influence is relational. It depends on trust, clarity, and consistency. When fear, guilt, insecurity, or shyness dominate a leader's internal posture, they shape the emotional environment experienced by others.[11]

Fear destabilises the emotional climate. Leaders may respond inconsistently or disproportionately to situations, making reactions difficult to anticipate. As a result, team members become cautious about sharing ideas, because they are uncertain how contributions will be received. Engagement shifts from curiosity to self-protection, and psychological safety begins to erode.[12]

Guilt weakens boundaries and obscures expectations. Leaders may accept responsibilities that should be delegated, hesitate to enforce standards, or avoid necessary limits. Over time, leadership becomes inconsistent. Teams struggle to understand priorities, authority lines, and expectations. Structure diminishes as leaders absorb too much responsibility and provide too little direction.[5]

Insecurity distorts interpretation. Initiative may be perceived as competition, commitment as threat, and competence as challenge. Leaders may respond by withholding information, delaying decisions, or avoiding delegation. These behaviours generate relational tension, reduce trust, and weaken confidence in leadership direction.[3]

Shyness restricts communication flow. Leaders may delay feedback, avoid difficult conversations, or withhold their thinking. While respect may remain, guidance diminishes. Teams operate with limited clarity and reduced connection, leading to distance rather than alignment.[10]

The result is a narrowed circle of influence. This occurs not because authority is absent, but because sustained contribution becomes difficult within an unstable emotional environment. Leadership influence strengthens when leaders provide clarity, predictability, and emotional stability for others.[13]

The Cost to Opportunities

When an internal leadership posture becomes a barrier, missed opportunities are often the first visible consequence. Although leaders' competence, commitment, and potential may attract opportunity, misalignment between internal posture and situational demands limits access. Opportunity is not allocated on capacity alone, but on perceived preparedness.[14]

Leaders who are qualified for advancement may remain positioned at the margins, not because opportunity is unavailable, but because their behaviour does not signal readiness for expanded influence.

This misalignment produces a pattern of exclusion. Leaders who are qualified for advancement may remain positioned at the margins, not because opportunity is unavailable, but because their behaviour does not signal readiness for expanded influence.

Research on leadership emergence shows that visibility, assertiveness, and confident participation strongly shape who is recognised as leadership material, often outweighing objective competence.[10]

Sponsorship that should be activated often remains dormant. Decision-makers tend to advance individuals they perceive as clear, decisive, and comfortable with authority, particularly in uncertain situations.

When internal posture constrains expression, leaders may be viewed as capable but not promotable, reliable but not strategic, trusted but not authoritative.[15]

Over time, leaders remain present within the organisation but peripheral to its influence. They are included in execution but excluded from decision-making, consulted but not entrusted with direction. This pattern reflects not a lack of contribution, but a sustained mismatch between internal posture and the behavioural signals required for opportunity activation.[3]

When left unexamined, this dynamic narrows professional trajectory. Leadership potential remains intact, but opportunity pathways close quietly as visibility, sponsorship, and strategic access shift toward those whose internal posture supports confident engagement with responsibility and exposure.[16]

The Cost to Strategic Contribution

Strategic leadership depends on cognitive availability, emotional regulation, and decisiveness. When leaders manage fear, guilt, or self-doubt internally, attentional resources are redirected away from strategic thinking toward self-monitoring and internal regulation. Research on cognitive load and self-regulation shows that ongoing internal vigilance significantly reduces working memory, executive function, and strategic judgment.[1,7,6]

Leaders may be physically present while mentally preoccupied with managing how they are perceived, justifying their position, or avoiding internal threat. This internal negotiation operates as a hidden tax on leadership capacity.

Sustained strategic contribution becomes difficult when internal resources are consumed by posture management rather than engagement with the work itself. Studies in leadership cognition demonstrate that emotional self-regulation demands reduce leaders' ability to process complexity, anticipate outcomes, and make timely decisions under pressure.[18,19] This result in diminished capability, but fragmented leadership output. Strategic contribution becomes inconsistent as internal posture repeatedly diverts attention away from sense-making, prioritisation, and execution. Over time, leaders contribute below their cognitive and strategic capacity, not because they lack insight, but because internal regulation demands continually draw energy away from leadership work.[19]

THE INTERNAL LEADERSHIP POSTURE COST INDICATOR (ILPCI)

A diagnostic to identify the extent to which your internal posture is costing you in leadership.

For each statement, rate how true it feels for you:

1 = Rarely true

2 = Sometimes true

3 = Often true

INTRAPERSONAL COSTS

(Leadership Capacity and Mental Health)

- I feel anxious, overwhelmed or pressured when responsibility increases.
- I overwork or push myself excessively because I feel I must prove myself.
- I hold back my contribution because I am unsure, I belong or will be accepted.
- Leadership opportunities drain me emotionally more than they inspire me.

Subtotal (Intrapersonal): ____

INTERPERSONAL COSTS

(Perception, Relationships and Influence)

- Others frequently misinterpret my confidence, intentions, or leadership clarity.
- I struggle to set and maintain clear boundaries without experiencing guilt.
- I interpret capable or enthusiastic colleagues as competitors rather than collaborators.
- I avoid or delay necessary conversations and

withhold timely feedback.

Subtotal (Interpersonal): ___

CONTEXTUAL COSTS

(Opportunities and Strategic Contribution)

- Opportunities arise, but I hesitate to act because I do not feel adequately prepared.
- I miss critical moments because I delay contributing or over analyse my input.
- I am present in influential spaces, but I do not exert corresponding influence within them.
- My ability to think and contribute strategically declines when my emotions are activated.

Subtotal (Contextual): __

TOTAL SCORE: _____

(Add your responses to all 12 statements.)

Minimum score: 12

Maximum score: 36

INTERPRETING YOUR SCORE

12–18: Early-stage cost

Your posture is just beginning to affect your leadership experience. Awareness at this stage can prevent deeper loss later.

19–27: Moderate cost

Your internal posture is actively shaping your opportunities, perceptions and influence.

28–36: Significant cost

Your internal leadership posture is costing you across all dimensions. Reconstruction will be essential if you want to rise into the next level of your leadership possibilities.

WHAT TO REMEMBER

- The cost of an unrevised posture is cumulative and multidimensional.
- Leadership capacity is not only about talent or ability.
- Leadership capacity is evaluated through behaviour, not intention.
- When internal barriers remain, a leader's capacity becomes misinterpreted by others.
- Influence weakens when the emotional environment becomes unstable.

CHAPTER FIVE

THE MECHANISM BEHIND THE INTERNAL LEADERSHIP POSTURE

The mechanisms described in this chapter draw on research in cognitive appraisal, self-evaluation, and behavioral expression in leadership to explain how internal leadership posture is sustained and reconstructed.[1,2,3]

The internal leadership posture is sustained by three underlying mechanisms. These mechanisms explain how emotional patterns formed in childhood translate into leadership behavior in adulthood. They shape how leaders interpret situations, evaluate themselves, and express leadership. These mechanisms are **interpretation**, **evaluation** and **expression.**

This understanding is important because leaders cannot reconstruct an internal posture without first recognizing the processes that sustain it.

Interpretation: How Leaders Make Sense of Leadership Moments

Interpretation is the mechanism through which leadership situations are understood, classified, and cognitively processed. It governs the meaning assigned to moments involving feedback, visibility, expectation, conflict, uncertainty, and opportunity. Interpretation precedes action and sets the emotional and cognitive tone for what follows.

Interpretation shapes how requests and instructions are appraised, how tone and intention are read, how social cues are understood. It determines how the demands of a moment are assessed, how significance is assigned to praise or critique, how the risks of visibility are judged, and how the implications of responsibility are interpreted. In this sense, interpretation constitutes the first internal response to a leadership situation. It functions as the lens through which reality is filtered.

Misinterpretation does not reflect the environment itself; it reflects the emotional posture through which the environment is interpreted. The same leadership moment can be experienced differently depending on the internal script.

These interpretive patterns are predictable. When internal leadership posture is rooted in fear, routine leadership demands are often interpreted as potential threats. When internal posture is shaped by guilt, requests are interpreted as obligations, leading to responsibility being assumed beyond what is required. When internal posture is shaped by insecurity, evaluation is interpreted as evidence of personal inadequacy, even in the absence of such evidence. When internal posture is shaped by shyness, participation is interpreted as exposure, leading to delay, minimisation, or avoidance. Such interpretations generate internal tension long before any outward action occurs.

Interpretation shapes how requests and instructions are appraised, how tone and intention are read, how social cues are understood.

Reconstruction begins with recalibrating the interpretive mechanism. This involves replacing inherited emotional appraisals with context-accurate assessments. A revised interpretive process enables leadership situations to be evaluated as they are, rather than through prior conditioning.

Evaluation determines the accuracy of self-assessment. When shaped by early emotional conditioning, this mechanism becomes inconsistent and unreliable

---

Evaluation: How Leaders Assess Capability and Legitimacy

Evaluation is the mechanism through which leaders assess competence, readiness, and legitimacy within leadership contexts. Evaluation governs internal judgements about contribution, preparedness, and belonging in leadership spaces.

Evaluation influences how effectiveness is judged, how readiness for responsibility is determined, how strengths and limitations are interpreted, how mistakes and feedback are processed, how decisions to engage or withdraw are made, and how legitimacy and authority are internally assessed.

Evaluation determines the accuracy of self-assessment. When shaped by early emotional conditioning, this mechanism becomes inconsistent and unreliable. Leaders shaped by insecurity often underestimate their capability despite evidence of competence. Leaders shaped by guilt frequently overestimate the level of responsibility required of them. Leaders shaped by fear underestimate their legitimacy and question their right to participate or decide. Leaders shaped by shyness overestimate the risk of judgement and consequently undervalue their readiness to contribute.

Distorted evaluation leads to hesitation, overcompensation, or withdrawal, not due to lack of ability, but because the internal assessment system is misaligned.

Reconstruction involves establishing a stable evaluation mechanism grounded in objective self-assessment and accurate recognition of capability. As evaluation becomes accurate leadership performance improves.

Expression: How Leadership Is Expressed

Expression is the mechanism through which internal leadership posture becomes observable in leadership behaviour. It governs the clarity, consistency, and effectiveness of communication and action in situations where leadership is required. Expression shapes the precision of verbal communication, the confidence with which ideas are presented, the firmness of boundaries, and the extent to which authority is recognised and respected. Expression is not limited to speaking, it encompasses the full range of behavioural signals through which leadership identity is conveyed, including tone, pace, posture, timing, decision-making, boundary setting, and behavioural follow-through.

When internal leadership posture is misaligned, expression is disrupted in predictable ways. When internal posture is rooted in fear, verbal and behavioural contribution is minimised, resulting in reduced visibility at critical moments. When internal posture is shaped by guilt, boundaries are weakened, which diminishes clarity and erodes authority. When internal posture is shaped by insecurity, communication becomes over-explained or excessively qualified, undermining confidence in leadership judgment. When internal posture is shaped by shyness, contribution is delayed or withdrawn, restricting influence and diminishing perceived capability.

Expression shapes the precision of verbal communication, confidence with which ideas are presented, firmness of boundaries, and the extent to which authority is recognised and respected.

Expression becomes effective when interpretation and evaluation are reconstructed. Accurate interpretation clarifies leadership moments, while secure self-assessment supports confidence in capability and legitimacy. Expression then emerges as the visible outcome of an aligned and functional internal posture.

WHAT TO REMEMBER

- The internal leadership posture is sustained by three mechanisms: Interpretation, Evaluation and Expression.
- Each mechanism translates early emotional conditioning into present leadership behaviour.
- Understanding the mechanisms is the foundation for building a healthier, more functional internal leadership posture.

PART THREE

THE RECONSTRUCT FRAMEWORK

How do I reconstruct the Internal Leadership

Posture?

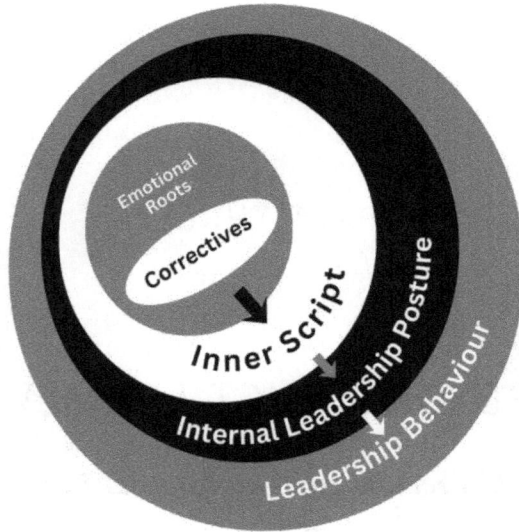

The Reconstructed Leadership Posture

RECONSTRUCT : The Internal Barriers That Keep Your Genius From Leading
(SheLeadership Advantage™ Book 1)

© 2026 PRINCESS-ANNE EMEKA-OBIAJUNWA

THE RECONSTRUCTED LEADERSHIP POSTURE

A reconstructed internal leadership posture is defined by four qualities. These qualities stabilise the mechanisms of interpretation, evaluation, and expression, producing a posture that can function effectively without reverting to childhood-shaped reflexes in the face of responsibility, visibility, and pressure.

Cultivate Courage
Apply Objectivity
Establish Identity- Grounding
Develop Self-Efficacy

The reconstructed leadership posture replaces emotionally driven reactions with deliberate, grounded leadership behavior. Courage interrupts the limiting effects of fear. Objectivity corrects distortions produced by guilt. Identity grounding stabilizes the uncertainty associated with insecurity. Self-efficacy strengthens expression where shyness would otherwise suppress it. Together, these qualities form an internal configuration that supports accurate interpretation, balanced self-evaluation, and consistent leadership expression.

This posture enables leaders to function with clarity and stability in environments that demand judgement, visibility, and influence.

CHAPTER SIX

CULTIVATE COURAGE

(COURAGE THE CORRECTIVE FOR FEAR)

Courage functions as the corrective quality by enabling intentional action in the presence of discomfort, rather than allowing perceived threat to govern behavior. Research indicates that leaders who demonstrate courage are perceived as more effective, trustworthy, and reliable under pressure.[1]

Moral courage is linked to clearer decision-making, follower confidence, and consistent ethical Behavior.[2] These findings position courage as a critical internal stabiliser in leadership.

Courage functions as the corrective quality by enabling intentional action in the presence of discomfort, rather than allowing perceived threat to govern behavior.

Courage strengthens expression by enabling timely contribution and decisive engagement. It supports the leader's capacity to participate fully in moments that require voice, initiative, or visibility. As courage increases, avoidance decreases. Leadership situations become more manageable because the leader is no longer governed by instinctive withdrawal but by deliberate action.

The following practices operationalize courage by restoring engagement where fear interrupts it.

Practice 1: Engage through Micro Exposure

Distortion

Fear inhibits expression by completing its avoidance cycle before action occurs. As a result, capable leaders delay engagement not because of inability, but because fear is allowed to run uninterrupted.

Principle

Action weakens fear when it occurs early and in controlled measure. Brief, repeatable engagement interrupts avoidance patterns and restores behavioural momentum.

Practice

Introduce small, deliberate acts of participation that are observable and time bound. Prioritise execution over performance. Examples include:

- Initiating the opening line of a necessary conversation, even if another person carries it forward.
- Presenting your offer, idea, or product to a single potential client rather than a full audience.
- Sharing one piece of expert content that demonstrates competence instead of attempting to build a full content strategy.

Why this works

Research on self-efficacy and action-based regulation shows that confidence increases through successful action initiation rather than prolonged preparation.[3,4] Micro exposure reduces psychological resistance while restoring a sense of agency, training the expression mechanism to act before fear completes its cycle.

Practice 2: Log Evidence

Distortion

Fear thrives in ambiguity. When outcomes are imagined rather than observed, threat is exaggerated and confidence erodes.

Principle

Confidence strengthens when interpretation is grounded in evidence. Recording actual outcomes replaces anticipated consequences with verifiable data, shifting judgment from assumption to assessment.

Practice

After each instance of participation, record four facts:

- the action you took
- what you feared would occur
- what actually occurred
- the difference between expectation and outcome

Keep the record factual and concise. Avoid interpretation or justification.

Why this works

Research on cognitive appraisal and self-regulation shows that behavioural confidence increases when individuals track real performance outcomes rather than relying on anticipated consequences.[5] Over time, this practice creates a personalised evidence base that recalibrates evaluation accuracy, weakens fear-based distortion, and builds confidence grounded in experience rather than anticipation.

Practice 3: Activate in Low-Stakes Situations

Distortion

Fear delays action by amplifying perceived threat. When engagement is postponed until conditions feel safe, avoidance patterns become reinforced.

Principle

Courage is strengthened through early, controlled action. Behavioural science shows that practising a behaviour where consequences are minimal allows the nervous system to develop familiarity and regulation before the behaviour is required in higher-stakes environments, consistent with exposure-based learning and inhibitory regulation of fear responses.[6,7]

Practice

Activate the required leadership behaviour first in a low-risk setting that closely mirrors the higher-risk context. For example:

• Practise stating your fees with a trusted colleague before stating them to a prospective client.

• Practise giving direct instruction in a home or volunteer context before delivering it at work.

• Practise articulating your opinion in a small group before doing so in a public forum.

Focus on execution rather than outcome.

Why this works

Low-stakes activation reduces threat reactivity while increasing behavioural readiness. Repeated rehearsal under manageable conditions builds familiarity and control, enabling clearer, more stable action when the stakes increase.

Practice 4: Reason Through Risk and Reward

Distortion

Fear distorts judgment by exaggerating potential cost and minimising potential benefit. As a result, avoidance is misinterpreted as safety.

Principle

Accurate decisions require comparative evaluation. Decision science shows that when risks and rewards are assessed side by side rather than emotionally, avoidance decreases and engagement becomes more likely.[8]

Practice

Before an action you are inclined to avoid, write out:
- the realistic risk of taking the action
- the realistic risk of avoiding the action
- the credible reward of taking the action
- the credible reward of avoiding the action

Force each outcome into concrete, plausible terms rather than imagined extremes.

Why this works

Comparative reasoning shifts interpretation from threat response to cognitive evaluation. For most women, this process reveals that avoidance carries the greater long-term cost. Recognising this weakens emotional resistance and prepares the interpretation mechanism to choose engagement rather than withdrawal.

WHAT TO REMEMBER

- **Apply courage** through action, not delay.

- **Engage early** and deliberately to interrupt avoidance.

- **Record outcomes** to replace assumption with evidence.

- **Practise leadership behaviours** in low-risk settings before high-stakes moments.

- **Compare the cost** of action with the cost of avoidance to guide decisions.

CHAPTER SEVEN

APPLY OBJECTIVITY

(OBJECTIVITY THE CORRECTIVE FOR GUILT)

Objectivity is the corrective quality because objectivity restores accuracy by grounding interpretation in verifiable information rather than emotional pressure. Objectivity aligns with cognitive reappraisal, an evidence-based emotion regulation strategy shown to reduce interpretive distortion, lower emotional reactivity, and support adaptive decision-making under pressure. [1,2]

Objectivity stabilizes evaluation by supporting accurate assessments of capacity, responsibility, and boundaries. Objectivity prevents the automatic assumption of excessive duty and supports decisions that are realistic, balanced, and aligned with actual leadership priorities.

Objectivity stabilizes evaluation by supporting accurate assessments of capacity, responsibility, and boundaries.

The following evidence-based tools strengthen objectivity, so leadership decisions remain grounded, proportionate, and sustainable over time.

Practice 5:

Audit Responsibility

Distortion

Guilt distorts responsibility by encouraging leaders to assume tasks, expectations, and emotional labour that fall outside their role. Over time, this leads to chronic overextension and blurred boundaries.

Principle

Accurate responsibility allocation requires structured evaluation. Research on executive functions and self-regulation shows that role clarity and deliberate decision rules improve judgment accuracy and limit overextension under high-demand conditions[3]

Practice

When a task, request, or expectation arises, evaluate it through three questions:

Is this my role?

Assess whether it aligns with your formal function, authority, or strategic contribution.

Is this my responsibility, or am I compensating for someone else's inaction?

Research shows that guilt-prone individuals are more likely to assume responsibility to manage relational or moral discomfort, even when the responsibility does not formally belong to them.[4]

What is the objective consequence if I release this?

In most cases, anticipated negative outcomes are emotional projections rather than evidence.

Why this works

The audit interrupts automatic over functioning by replacing emotional obligation with structural clarity. It recalibrates interpretation, strengthening accuracy around what you carry, what you release, and why.

Practice 6:
Decide Using Neutral Criteria

Distortion

Guilt accelerates agreement. Under moral or relational pressure, leaders default to rapid yes-responses that bypass evaluation and inflate responsibility.

Principle

Objectivity requires pre-set conditions. Decisions made against neutral criteria are less vulnerable to emotional pressure and judgment noise.[5,6]

Practice

Before accepting any request, pause and evaluate it against three criteria:

• Necessity: Is this essential to your role or the intended   outcome?
• Ownership: Is this genuinely yours to carry, or simply   available   for   you   to   absorb?
• Sustainability: Can this be maintained without compromising   higher   priorities   or   core responsibilities?

Why this works

Decision hygiene research shows that neutral,

predefined criteria reduce emotional distortion and inconsistency in judgment, particularly in high-responsibility environments.[7] This practice trains the evaluation mechanism to assign responsibility based on necessity and capacity rather than guilt.

Practice 7 : Draw the Capacity Line

Distortion

Guilt blurs boundaries by normalising overload. Tasks accumulate without distinction, and excessive responsibility is misinterpreted as commitment.

Principle

Proportional workload requires visible limits. When responsibilities remain internal and unstructured, emotional bias interferes with accurate evaluation.

Practice

Create a visual boundary by dividing your workload into three horizontal sections:

1. **Core responsibilities**

   Non-negotiable tasks central to your role and mandate.

2. **Secondary duties**

   Responsibilities that fluctuate depending on context or season.

3. **Optional support tasks**

   Tasks that are negotiable, deferrable, or delegable. Place every active task into one category. Any task placed in the third section must be renegotiated, delegated, or released.

Why this works

Research on cognitive offloading shows that externalising information improves judgment accuracy and reduces emotional interference.[8]

Visual categorisation forces objective evaluation and exposes overload that guilt often disguises as normal.

Practice 8: Apply the Proportional Effort Rule

Distortion

Guilt distorts effort allocation by inflating investment in tasks that carry emotional pressure but limited strategic value. As a result, leaders overcommit energy to low-impact work while depleting capacity needed for higher-priority responsibilities.

Principle

Effective leadership requires alignment between effort and value. Research in organisational psychology shows that misalignment between demands and available resources reduces effectiveness and accelerates burnout, particularly when effort is driven by obligation rather than importance.[9]

Practice

Evaluate each active task against two dimensions:
• Strategic importance
• Effort required

Where effort consistently exceeds importance, deliberately reduce the level of investment to match the task's actual value. This may involve limiting time spent, lowering performance intensity, or renegotiating scope.

Why this works

The proportional effort rule recalibrates the evaluation system, ensuring energy is allocated according to impact rather than guilt. By restoring alignment between effort and value, it preserves capacity for work that genuinely matters and prevents overextension disguised as responsibility.

WHAT TO REMEMBER

- **Anchor decisions** on verifiable information.
- **Audit responsibility** to prevent over-functioning.
- **Decide** using neutral criteria.
- **Assess capacity** before taking on duty.

CHAPTER EIGHT

ESTABLISH IDENTITTY GROUNDING

(Identity Grounding, the Corrective for Insecurity)

Identity grounding functions as the corrective quality by establishing internal stability through a clear and anchored sense of self, independent of fluctuating environments or external validation. Identity grounding aligns with research on authentic leadership, which identifies self-awareness, internalised values and relational transparency as predictors of effective and consistent leadership behaviour.[1]

Identity grounding functions as the corrective quality by establishing internal stability through a clear and anchored sense of self, independent of fluctuating environments or external validation.

Leaders with a grounded sense of identity demonstrate clearer judgement, greater behavioral consistency, and receive higher levels of trust from followers. [1,2]

Identity grounding stabilises evaluation by providing a reliable internal reference point that reduces self-doubt and strengthens legitimacy.[2,3] Identity grounding supports decisions that reflect established values rather than insecurity, enabling the leader to act from clarity across complex or high pressure environments.

The following practices stabilise identity by clarifying self-definition, consolidating internal authority, and reducing dependence on external evaluation.

Practice 9: Separate Role from Self

Distortion

Insecurity intensifies when leaders fuse identity with role performance. When evaluation or challenge arises, normal role-based feedback is misinterpreted as personal deficiency.

Principle

Identity stability requires separation between who you are and what the role demands. Research on role identification and role fusion shows that over-identifying with a role heightens self-doubt and reduces resilience under scrutiny.[4]

Practice

Create two distinct lists:

Self (non-role-based attributes)

This includes your values, capabilities, strengths, convictions, knowledge, and internal drivers that remain consistent across contexts.

Role (context-dependent expectations)

This includes your tasks, deliverables, functions, and competencies required in your current leadership environment.

Review the lists separately.

Why this works

Separating role from self prevents leadership challenges from being interpreted as personal inadequacy. It stabilises internal evaluation by anchoring identity in enduring attributes rather than fluctuating role expectations, reducing insecurity across changing contexts.

Practice 10: Define Self Through Evidence

Distortion

Insecurity persists when self-definition is vague or impression-based. Without concrete reference points, internal evaluation becomes unstable and overly sensitive to feedback, comparison, or context.

Principle

Identity stability depends on self-concept clarity. Research indicates that identity becomes more coherent and resilient when self-definitions are specific, consistent, and grounded in evidence rather than subjective interpretation. [5]

Practice

Create an evidence-based self-definition by documenting:

- three skills you have repeatedly demonstrated
- three strengths others consistently confirm
- three outcomes you have produced reliably
- three environments in which you perform strongly

  Treat these as factual anchors, not affirmations.

Why this works

Concrete evidence stabilises internal evaluation by

replacing emotional inference with verifiable data. Over time, the mind learns to reference demonstrated capability rather than fluctuating self-doubt, strengthening identity grounding across contexts.

Practice 11: Establish Internal Authority

Distortion

Insecurity weakens decision-making by shifting authority outward. Leaders shaped by insecurity rely excessively on approval, comparison, or consensus to validate their right to act.

Principle

Authority stabilises when it is internally legitimised. Research on self-affirmation shows that grounding decisions in evidence-based self-worth improves performance and reduces defensiveness under evaluative pressure.[6]

Practice

Create three internal authority statements using the following structure: "I have the authority to ___ because I consistently demonstrate ___." For example,

"I have the authority to contribute strategically because I consistently identify patterns and propose workable solutions."
Use these statements to interrupt comparison and reassert evaluative stability in moments of doubt or scrutiny.

Why this works

Internal authority statements relocate legitimacy from external approval to demonstrated capability. This strengthens internal legitimacy, stabilises evaluation, and reduces comparison-driven self-doubt in leadership decisions

Practice 12: Decide From Identity

Distortion

Insecurity compromises decision-making by shifting evaluation toward relational pressure, approval-seeking, or avoidance. Choices become reactive rather than internally coherent.

Principle

Identity-grounded leadership requires decisions that align with internal values and self-definition. Research on authentic leadership shows that value-congruent decision-making produces greater behavioural consistency and reduces anxiety under scrutiny.[1]

Practice

Before making a leadership decision, evaluate it using four questions:

1. Does this action reflect my values?
2. Does this align with my long-term identity as a leader?
3. Is this choice driven by clarity or by insecurity?
4. What evidence supports my capability to execute this decision?

Why this works

This filter anchors evaluation in identity rather than approval or avoidance. By grounding decisions in values and demonstrated capability, it stabilises judgment and reinforces internal authority under pressure.

WHAT TO REMEMBER

- **Separate identity from role** to prevent insecurity from distorting judgement.
- **Define identity using evidence**, not impression or feedback alone.
- **Establish internal authority** before seeking external validation.
- **Make decisions that align** with values and demonstrated capability.
- **Anchor leadership action in identity**, not approval or comparison.

CHAPTER NINE

DEVELOP SELF-EFFICACY

(Self-efficacy, the Corrective for Shyness)

Self-efficacy functions as the corrective quality by supporting confident action, influence, and effective performance in leadership situations.

In leadership contexts, self-efficacy is strongly associated with higher performance, greater resilience, and increased willingness to engage when decisions, competence, or authority are being assessed.[1,2] Leaders with higher self-efficacy demonstrate clearer communication, greater behavioural consistency and stronger initiative.[1,3] Self-efficacy strengthens expression by increasing confidence in the ability to contribute effectively. It reduces hesitation, supports timely engagement and allows the leader's insight and competence to become visible. [1,3,4]

Self-efficacy functions as the corrective quality by supporting confident action, influence, and effective performance in leadership situations.

As self-efficacy increases, expression becomes consistent and leadership presence becomes stable across environments.

The following practices build self-efficacy by

recalibrating the expression mechanism, increasing behavioural readiness, and reducing the internal inhibition that limits leadership presence.

Practice 13: Map Mastery

Distortion

Shyness distorts self-perception by minimising or overlooking demonstrated competence. Capability is forgotten, dismissed, or treated as incidental.

Principle

Self-efficacy strengthens through mastery experiences. Research shows that repeated recognition of successful performance is the most powerful source of efficacy beliefs.[3]

Practice

Identify three to five leadership actions you perform well. For each, record:

• the behaviour

• a concrete example where you executed it effectively

• the outcome produced

• the capability demonstrated

Treat this as an evidence record, not self-appraisal.

Why this works

Mapping mastery replaces emotional self-doubt with factual competence. It trains the expression mechanism to anticipate successful action rather than inhibition.

Practice 14: Increase Expression Incrementally

Distortion

Shyness suppresses contribution by associating visibility with excessive evaluative threat. Expression is delayed until confidence feels complete.

Principle

Behavioural confidence develops through graded exposure. Research shows that incremental rehearsal increases performance under evaluation without triggering overwhelming self-consciousness. [5]

Practice

Select one expression behaviour you tend to avoid.

Design three ascending levels of the same behaviour:

- Level 1: very low visibility
- Level 2: moderate visibility
- Level 3: higher visibility

Progress sequentially. Do not skip levels.

Why this works

Incremental expression builds behavioural readiness before emotional readiness. This is the core mechanism of self-efficacy development.

Practice 15: Pair Competence with Visibility

Distortion

Shyness disrupts expression by separating visibility from competence. Being seen is interpreted as risky even when capability is already established, leading leaders to withhold contribution despite readiness.

Principle

Self-efficacy increases when visible action is taken in areas of demonstrated strength. Research shows that efficacy strengthens when individuals act publicly in domains where competence is already high, allowing successful performance to occur under observation rather than avoidance.[3,6]

Practice

Identify one capability in which you are already confident and deliberately link it to a visible leadership action. For example, if your strength lies in analysis, take responsibility for summarising the discussion. If writing is a strength, present the written recommendation you prepared. If you ask strong questions, lead the questioning segment. If organisation is a core capability, open the meeting by outlining the agenda.

Why this works

This pairing anchors visibility to competence rather than fear. The expression mechanism learns to associate being seen with successful execution, not threat, reducing inhibition and strengthening confidence in future visible leadership moments.

Practice 16: Consolidate Success After Action

Distortion

Shyness allows successful expression to occur without integration. Action happens, but its significance is not consolidated, leaving future expectations unchanged.

Principle

Performance strengthens self-efficacy only when success is cognitively integrated into future expectations. Research on efficacy–performance spirals show that explicitly consolidating successful behaviour stabilises confidence and increases subsequent engagement. [6]

Practice

After a leadership expression moment, identify one capability you exercised successfully and state it explicitly. Then identify one condition under which it worked.

Do not analyse further. Do not evaluate performance quality.

Why this works

This practice converts action into expectation. By consolidating success at the level of capability rather than outcome, it stabilises self-efficacy and strengthens future expression without reactivating self-monitoring.

WHAT TO REMEMBER

• **Build confidence** through documented mastery.

• **Increase expression** by taking simple steps at a time.

• **Be visible** where competence is already established.

•**Consolidate successful action** to stabilise self-efficacy.

END NOTES

Chapter One

1. Murphy, S. E. and Johnson, S. K. (2011) *The benefits of a long lens approach to leader development: Understanding the seeds of leadership.* Leadership Quarterly, 22(3), pp. 459–470.

2. Komives, S. R., Owen, J. E., Longerbeam, S. D., Mainella, F. C. and Osteen, L. (2005) *Developing a leadership identity: A grounded theory.* Journal of College Student Development, 46(6), pp. 593–611.

3. Lord, R. G. and Hall, R. J. (2005) 'Identity, deep structure and the development of leadership

skill', *Leadership Quarterly*, 16(4), pp. 591–615.

Chapter Two

1. Derue, D.S., Nahrgang, J.D., Wellman, N.E. and Humphrey, S.E. (2011) Trait and behavioral theories of leadership: An integration and meta-analytic test of their relative validity. *Personnel Psychology*. [Online] 64 (1), 7–52.

2. Fleishman, E. A., Mumford, M. D., Zaccaro, S. J., Levin, K. Y., Korotkin, A. L. and Hein, M. B. (1991) Taxonomic efforts in the description of leader behavior: A synthesis and functional interpretation. *The Leadership Quarterly*. [Online] 2 (4), 245–287.

3. Lord, R. G. and Hall, R. J. (2005) Identity, deep structure and the development of leadership skills. *The Leadership Quarterly*. [Online] 16 (4), 591–615.

4. Hannah, S. T., Walumbwa, F. O. and Fry, L. W.

(2011) Leadership in action: A systems perspective of leadership. *Journal of Organizational Behavior*. [Online] 32 (3), 269–290.

5. George, J. M. (2000) Emotions and leadership: The role of emotional intelligence. *Human Relations*. [Online] 53 (8), 1027–1055.

6. Hubbart, J. A. (2024) Understanding and mitigating leadership fear-based behaviors on employee and organizational success. *Administrative Sciences*. [Online] 14 (9), 225.

7. Schaumberg, R. L. and Flynn, F. J. (2012) Uneasy lies the head that wears the crown: The link between guilt proneness and leadership. *Journal of Personality and Social Psychology*. [Online] 103 (2), 327–342.

8. Petriglieri, J. L. (2011) Under threat: Responses to and the consequences of threats to individuals' identities. *Academy of Management Review*. [Online] 36 (4), 641–662.

9. Judge, T. A., Bono, J. E., Ilies, R. and Gerhardt,

M. W. (2002) Personality and leadership: A qualitative and quantitative review. *Journal of Applied Psychology.* [Online] 87 (4), 765–780.

10. Escobar Vega, C. et al. (2025) The Development of Implicit Leadership Theories During Childhood: A Reconceptualization Through the Lens of Overlapping Waves Theory. *Psychological Review.* [Online] 132 (3), 719–743.

11. Ryan, N. F. et al. (2024) A qualitative study unpacking the leader identity development process taking a multi-domain approach. *Leadership & Organization Development Journal.* [Online] 45 (4), 602–618.

12. Owen, J. E. (2023) Deepening leadership identity development. *New Directions for Student Leadership.* [Online] 2023 (178), 11–20.

13. Ely, R. J. et al. (2011) Taking gender into account: Theory and design for women's leadership development. *Academy of Management Learning & Education.* [Online] 10

(3), 474–493.

Chapter Three

1. Ely, R. J. et al. (2011) *Taking gender into account: Theory and design for women's leadership development.* Academy of Management Learning & Education. [Online] 10 (3), 474–493.
2. Eagly, A. H., Wood, W. and Diekman, A. B. (2000) *Social Role Theory of Sex Differences and Similarities: A Current Appraisal.* In: Trautner, H. M. and Eckes, T. (eds.) The Developmental Social Psychology of Gender. Psychology Press, 123–174.

Chapter Four

1. Hannah, S. T., Walumbwa, F. O. and Fry, L. W. (2011) Leadership in action: A systems perspective of leadership. *Journal of*

Organizational Behavior. [Online] 32 (3), 269–290.

2. Maslach, C. and Leiter, M. P. (2008) Early predictors of job burnout and engagement. *Journal of Applied Psychology.* [Online] 93 (3), 498–512.

3. Petriglieri, J. L. (2011) Under threat: Responses to and the consequences of threats to individuals' identities. *Academy of Management Review.* [Online] 36 (4), 641–662.

4. Hobfoll, S. E. (2001) The influence of culture, community, and the nested self in the stress process: Advancing conservation of resources theory. *Applied Psychology.* [Online] 50 (3), 337–421.

5. Schaumberg, R. L. and Flynn, F. J. (2012) Uneasy lies the head that wears the crown: The link between guilt proneness and leadership. *Journal of Personality and Social Psychology.* [Online] 103 (2), 327–342.

6. Hofmann, W., Schmeichel, B. J. and Baddeley, A. D. (2012) Executive functions and self-regulation. *Trends in Cognitive Sciences.* [Online] 16 (3), 174–180.

7. Fleishman, E. A., Mumford, M. D., Zaccaro, S. J., Levin, K. Y., Korotkin, A. L. and Hein, M. B. (1991) Taxonomic efforts in the description of leader behavior: A synthesis and functional interpretation. *The Leadership Quarterly.* [Online] 2 (4), 245–287.

8. DeRue, D. S., Nahrgang, J. D., Wellman, N. E. and Humphrey, S. E. (2011) Trait and behavioral theories of leadership: An integration and meta-analytic test of their relative validity. *Personnel Psychology.* [Online] 64 (1), 7–52.

9. Judge, T. A., Bono, J. E., Ilies, R. and Gerhardt, M. W. (2002) Personality and leadership: A qualitative and quantitative review. *Journal of Applied Psychology.* [Online] 87 (4), 765–780.

10. Dirks, K. T. and Ferrin, D. L. (2002) Trust in leadership: Meta-analytic findings and implications for research and practice. *Journal of Applied Psychology*. [Online] 87 (4), 611–628.

11. Edmondson, A. (1999) Psychological safety and learning behavior in work teams. *Administrative Science Quarterly*. [Online] 44 (2), 350–383.

12. George, J. M. (2000) Emotions and leadership: The role of emotional intelligence. *Human Relations*. [Online] 53 (8), 1027–1055.

13. DeRue, D. S. and Ashford, S. J. (2010) Who will lead and who will follow? A social process of leadership identity construction in organizations. *Academy of Management Review*. [Online] 35 (4), 627–647.

14. Ibarra, H., Ely, R. J. and Kolb, D. M. (2013) Women rising: The unseen barriers. *Harvard Business Review*. [Online] 91 (9), 60–66.

15. Ashford, S. J., DeRue, D. S. and Wellman, N. (2008) The role of self-regulation in developing leaders: A longitudinal field study. *Journal of Applied Psychology.* [Online] 93 (1), 29–44.

16. Baumeister, R. F., Vohs, K. D. and Tice, D. M. (2007) The strength model of self-control. *Current Directions in Psychological Science.* [Online] 16 (6), 351–355.

17. Hannah, S. T., Woolfolk, R. L. and Lord, R. G. (2009) Leader self-regulation: A framework for understanding leadership effectiveness under stress. *The Leadership Quarterly.* [Online] 20 (5), 680–699.

18. Lerner, J. S., Li, Y., Valdesolo, P. and Kassam, K. S. (2015) Emotion and decision making. *Annual Review of Psychology.* [Online] 66, 799–823.

19. Kahneman, D., Sibony, O. and Sunstein, C. R. (2021) *Noise: A Flaw in Human Judgment.* London: Little, Brown Spark.

Chapter Five

1. Gross, J.J. and John, O.P., 2003. Individual differences in two emotion regulation processes: Implications for affect, relationships, and well-being. *Journal of Personality and Social Psychology*, 85(2), pp.348–362.

2. Bandura, A., 1997. *Self-efficacy: The exercise of control*. New York: Freeman.

3. Fleishman, E.A., Mumford, M.D., Zaccaro, S.J., Levin, K.Y., Korotkin, A.L. and Hein, M.B., 1991. Taxonomic efforts in the description of leader behavior: A synthesis and functional interpretation. *The Leadership Quarterly*, 2(4), pp.245–287.

Chapter Six

1. Hannah, S. T., Walumbwa, F. O. and Fry, L. W. (2011) Leadership in action: A systems perspective of leadership. *Journal of Organizational Behavior.* [Online] 32 (3), 269–290.

2. Sekerka, L. E. and Bagozzi, R. P. (2007) Moral courage in the workplace: Moving to and from the desire and decision to act. *Business Ethics: A European Review.* [Online] 16 (2), 132–149.

3. Bandura, A. (1997) *Self-efficacy: The exercise of control.* New York: Freeman.

4. Bandura, A. and Wood, R. (1989) Effect of perceived controllability and performance standards on self-regulation of complex decision making. *Journal of Personality and Social Psychology.* [Online] 56 (5), 805–814.

5. Gross, J. J. and John, O. P. (2003) Individual differences in two emotion regulation processes: Implications for affect, relationships, and well-being. *Journal of*

Personality and Social Psychology. [Online] 85 (2), 348–362.

6. Foa, E. B. and Kozak, M. J. (1986) Emotional processing of fear: Exposure to corrective information. *Psychological Bulletin.* [Online] 99 (1), 20–35.

7. Craske, M. G., Treanor, M., Conway, C. C., Zbozinek, T. and Vervliet, B. (2014) Maximizing exposure therapy: An inhibitory learning approach. *Behaviour Research and Therapy.* [Online] 58, 10–23.

8. Kahneman, D. and Tversky, A. (1979) Prospect theory: An analysis of decision under risk. *Econometrica.* [Online] 47 (2), 263–291.

Chapter Seven

1. Gross, J. J. and John, O. P. (2003) Individual differences in two emotion regulation processes: Implications for affect,

relationships, and well-being. *Journal of Personality and Social Psychology.* [Online] 85 (2), 348–362.

2. Troy, A. S., Wilhelm, F. H., Shallcross, A. J. and Mauss, I. B. (2010) Seeing the silver lining: Cognitive reappraisal ability moderates the relationship between stress and depressive symptoms. *Emotion.* [Online] 10 (6), 783–795.

3. Hofmann, W., Schmeichel, B. J. and Baddeley, A. D. (2012) Executive functions and self-regulation. *Trends in Cognitive Sciences.* [Online] 16 (3), 174–180.

4. Schaumberg, R. L. and Flynn, F. J. (2012) Uneasy lies the head that wears the crown: The link between guilt proneness and leadership. *Journal of Personality and Social Psychology.* [Online] 103 (2), 327–342.

5. Bazerman, M. H. and Moore, D. A. (2012) *Judgment in managerial decision making.* Hoboken, NJ: John Wiley & Sons.

6. Kahneman, D., Sibony, O. and Sunstein, C. R. (2021) *Noise: A flaw in human judgment.* London: Hachette UK.

7. Kahneman, D. and Tversky, A. (1979) Prospect theory: An analysis of decision under risk. *Econometrica.* [Online] 47 (2), 263–291.

8. Risko, E. F. and Gilbert, S. J. (2016) Cognitive offloading. *Trends in Cognitive Sciences.* [Online] 20 (9), 676–688.

9. Maslach, C. and Leiter, M. P. (2008) Early predictors of job burnout and engagement. *Journal of Applied Psychology.* [Online] 93 (3), 498–512.

Chapter Eight

1. Walumbwa, F. O., Avolio, B. J., Gardner, W. L., Wernsing, T. S. and Peterson, S. J. (2008) Authentic leadership: Development and

validation of a theory-based measure. *Journal of Management.* [Online] 34 (1), 89–126.

2. Campbell, J. D., Trapnell, P. D., Heine, S. J., Katz, I. M., Lavallee, L. F. and Lehman, D. R. (1996) Self-concept clarity: Measurement, personality correlates, and cultural boundaries. *Journal of Personality and Social Psychology.* [Online] 70 (1), 141–156.

3. Petriglieri, J. L. (2011) Under threat: Responses to and the consequences of threats to individuals' identities. *Academy of Management Review.* [Online] 36 (4), 641–662.

4. Ashforth, B. E. (2001) *Role transitions in organizational life: An identity-based perspective.* Mahwah, NJ: Lawrence Erlbaum Associates.

5. Cohen, G. L. and Sherman, D. K. (2014) The psychology of change: Self-affirmation and social psychological intervention. *Annual Review of Psychology.* [Online] 65 (1), 333–371.

Chapter Nine

1. Hannah, S. T., Avolio, B. J., Luthans, F. and Harms, P. D. (2008) Leadership efficacy: Review and future directions. *The Leadership Quarterly.* [Online] 19 (6), 669–692.

2. Hoyt, C. L. and Blascovich, J. (2007) Leadership efficacy and women leaders' responses to stereotype activation. *Group Processes & Intergroup Relations.* [Online] 10 (4), 595–616.

3. Bandura, A. (1997) *Self-efficacy: The exercise of control.* New York: Freeman.

4. Paglis, L.L. and Green, S.G., 2002. Leadership self-efficacy and managers' motivation for leading change. *Journal of Organizational Behavior: The International Journal of Industrial, Occupational and Organizational Psychology and Behavior,* 23(2), pp.215-235.

5. Rachman, S. J. (2004) Fear and courage: A psychological perspective. *Social Research.* [Online] 71 (1), 149–176.

6. Lindsley, D. H., Brass, D. J. and Thomas, J. B. (1995) Efficacy-performing spirals: A multilevel perspective. *Academy of Management Review.* [Online] 20 (3), 645–678.

ABOUT THE AUTHOR

Princess Anne is a leadership expert, keynote speaker, and corporate consultant who strengthens leadership effectiveness and organizational excellence across various sectors. She is known for developing inclusive leadership systems and performance-driven talent strategies, with a specialized focus on gender equity.

With two decades of experience across education, nonprofit, public sector, and corporate environments, she designs and delivers transformative strategies that drive meaningful change at both organizational and individual levels.

Through the SheLeadership Framework™, a

culturally intelligent, gender-aware model, Princess Anne partners with organizations to strengthen leadership pipelines, build equitable cultures, audit bias in talent processes, embed DEI KPIs into corporate strategy, design bespoke leadership development programmes, accelerate high-potential talent, and advise boards and C-suite on equity governance.

She delivers leadership development for leaders and teams through workshops, cohort-based intensives, immersive learning experiences, retreats and coaching that build clarity, capacity, and strategic influence. She also provides dedicated pathways to support women navigating systemic leadership barriers and advancing into leadership positions across government, education, technology, and business.

Committed to social impact, Princess founded the Birthplace Empowerment Foundation, which has transformed thousands of youths and women through mentoring, humanitarian services, and education in underserved communities.

A prolific author, certified NLP practitioner, and theologian, Princess Anne's books explore the intersection of Leadership, Personal development, Faith, and social change.

CONNECT WITH PRINCESS

Website

https://princessemekaobiajunwa.com/

https://thesheleadership.com/

https://birthplacefoundation.org/

Social Media

Linkedin

https://www.linkedin.com/in/princess-emeka-obiajunwa/

Facebook: Princess Emeka-Obiajunwa

Instagram: Princess Emeka-Obiajunwa

YouTube:

https://www.youtube.com/@PrincessEmekaObiajunwa

OTHER BOOKS BY PRINCESS-ANNE

BOOKS ARE AVAILABLE ON HER WEBSITE

AND ON AMAZON

OTHER BOOKS BY PRINCESS-ANNE
BOOKS ARE AVAILABLE ON HER WEBSITE
AND ON AMAZON

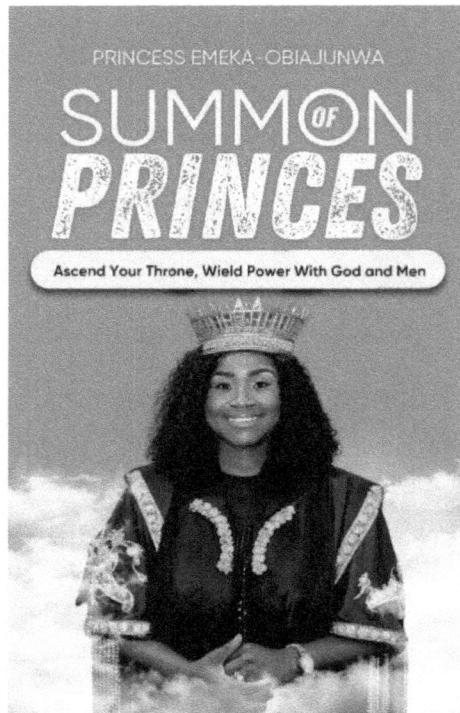

PRINCESS EMEKA-OBIAJUNWA

SUMMON OF PRINCES

Ascend Your Throne, Wield Power With God and Men

In this life-changing book, **Summon of Princes**, you will:

Discover your identity and responsibility as God's Prince. Identify your God-assigned throne in the spirit and how to effectively wield its influence in the earthly realm. Learn to counter the serpent's tactics to undermine your authority, as he did with Adam, and overcome as Jesus did. Navigate the three gates to your throne, and the consecrations required to pass the tests at these gates. Explore the five dimensions of kingdom government for man. Surrender to the six necessary death processes that unlock the full glory within your spirit.

Prepare to rule nations with Jesus during this time, His millennial reign, and beyond.

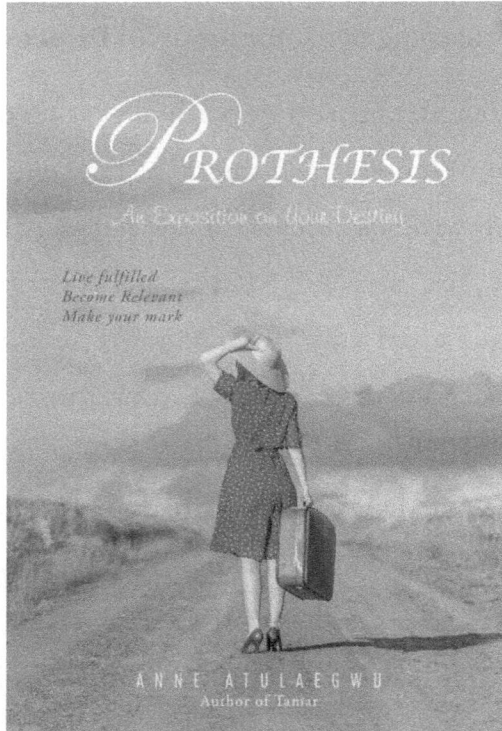

In the book Prothesis you will learn to let God lead you into His flawless purpose for you, learn to let God lead you into His flawless purpose for you, understand the link between your gifts, talents and your purpose, and be empowered to make your mark, be relevant and live fulfilled.

This book challenges you to move from where you are to where you ought to be - a glorious fulfilling life!

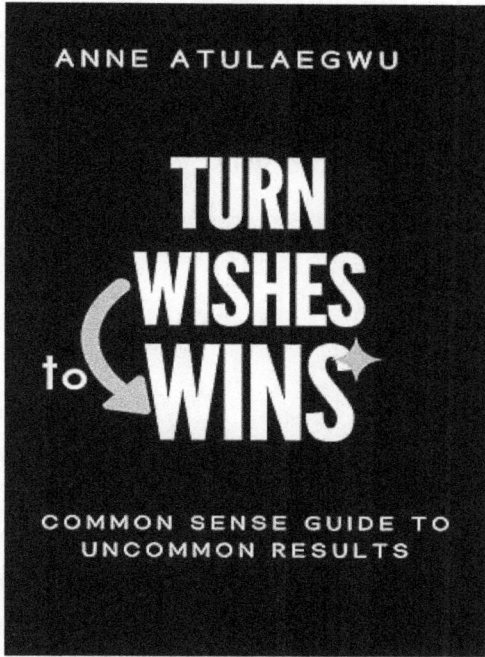

ANNE ATULAEGWU

TURN WISHES to WINS

COMMON SENSE GUIDE TO UNCOMMON RESULTS

In the first part of **Turn Wishes to Win,** *Rule Storms*, I will guide you through overcoming the five most common and destructive storms of life. These challenges hinder your desires, thwart your wishes, and prevent you from achieving the success you deserve.

In the second part, *Execute Missions*, I will reveal the eight essential powers that underpin every notable achievement.

You will be equipped to execute your goals with effectiveness and excellence. Say goodbye to regrets, wasted resources, and misplaced priorities. No more buried hopes.

In the third part, *Grab Gold*, I share seven key qualities of those who turn wishes into wins. You will learn how to transform your dreams into reality and live fully and unapologetically fulfilled.

Get started on creating your best life yet.

7 SIGNS YOU ARE SABOTAGING YOUR FUTURE

AND HOW TO RESCUE IT

ANNE ATULAEGWU

Many people think it is okay to just have a dream and work hard or smart (whatever your school of thought).

However, success in all of its holistic definition is more than that!

In this book, Anne Atulaegwu interestingly shows you 7 warning signs that you might be ruining all you are currently working for and helps you identify the triggers associated with self-sabotaging behaviours.

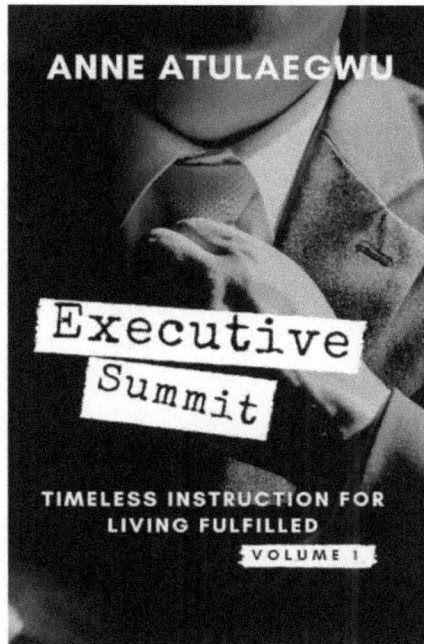

Living in times when days fly by fast, technology gets upgraded per second and last night's most trendy dress takes the back seat by morning; we sure need some stability for our souls without losing touch with the times. If you have ever desired a richer, fuller life that includes material blessings and the true riches of eternal worth? Then you must become wise- a person who heeds instruction.

In the Executive summit series, Anne Atulaegwu serves you a good doze of stability and wisdom required for you to live fulfilled, make you mark where it matters most and retain relevance in an ever-changing world.

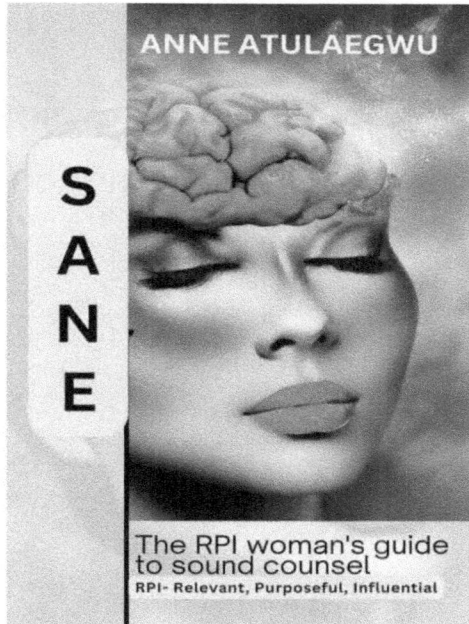

SANE is the first of a series; designed like a magazine with illustrative images to help you capture its message.

In this volume, you will learn to overcome the fear of new beginnings, get over depression, do exploits while being approachable for marriage, step into your purpose and impart lives, balance school, work and ministry, and know the difference between God's voice and your mind.

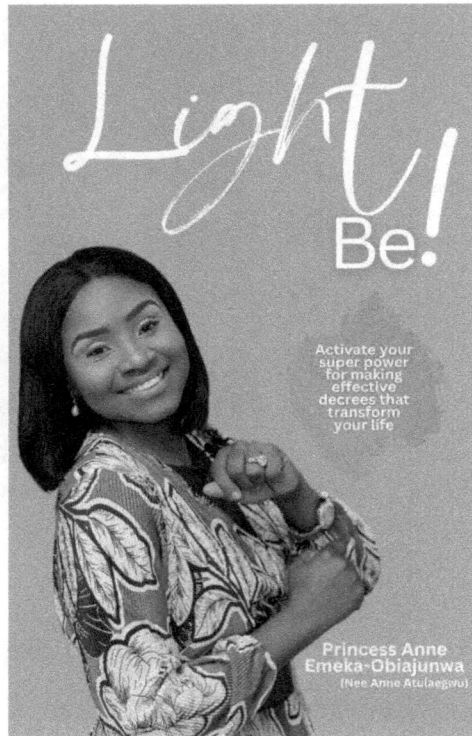

Light Be: Life invites us into chapters where we must craft significance from emptiness, forge substance from the void, and reorder peace amidst chaos. The difference between those who effectively do these and the ones who struggle is the ability to make enduring decrees that compel change. The compelling force of enduring decrees has long been attributed exclusively to "powerful" prophets. But it is not just for them; you were designed for and can have this kind of influence too.

"Light Be" calls you into a future where you not only navigate change but become its architect.

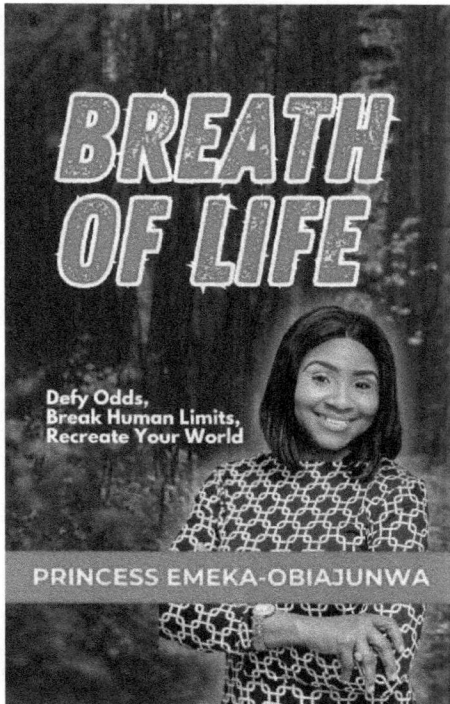

In Breath of Life, Princess-Anne Emeka-Obiajunwa challenges your current mindset and ignites new

possibilities you have never envisioned for your life. This book reveals how to turn moments of emptiness and discouragement into extraordinary triumphs and victories.

By exploring the themes of life, death, and immortality, Princess-Anne equips you with the essential tools to:

- **Break the five limitations of human nature** that hinder your life's true beauty.

- **Harness the creative power of eternal life** to transform your world.

- **Uncover the three indicators of immortality** residing within you.

- **Engage the eight operations of the life-giving Spirit** that empower you to overcome obstacles and unleash your glory.

- **Unlock the extraordinary ability** to defy the odds through intimacy with God.

Open the pages and get started on your testimony of a transformed life today

Godly Meditation
COURSE
NOW ON
udemy
GODLY MEDITATION
Princess Anne Emeka-Obiajunwa
PRINCESS ANNE
Emeka-Obiajunwa
www.anneemekaobiajunwa.com/courses

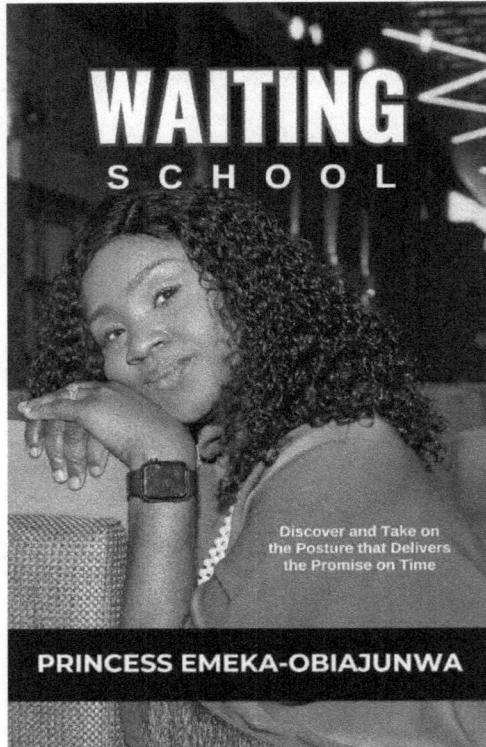

In Waiting School, Princess-Anne offers you a compassionate, insightful guide for navigating life's inevitable waiting seasons. With warmth, humour, and vulnerability, she shares relatable stories of her own experiences—stories of academic disappointment, longing for love, and waiting for a child amid unexpected challenges.

Each page unveils life-changing insights that illuminate dark paths.

Inside, you will discover:

- The six mysteries behind waiting
- The five core purposes that waiting fulfils
- The seven postures that influence the timing of your breakthrough

Waiting School is here to uplift you, strengthen your faith, and help fast-track your journey.

Dive in!

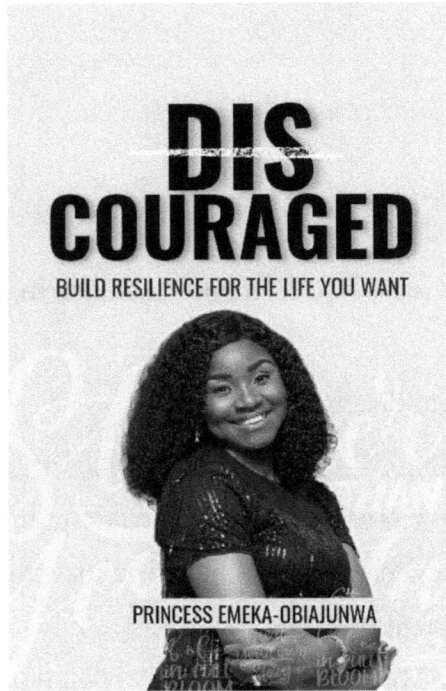

DIS COURAGED
BUILD RESILIENCE FOR THE LIFE YOU WANT
PRINCESS EMEKA-OBIAJUNWA

Discouraged is an honest and heartfelt look at the lives of people who hit rock bottom yet found hope and restoration when it seemed out of reach. These are the stories of people we recognize—Leah, the overlooked wife longing for love; Peter, the evangelist haunted by shame; and Hagar, the abandoned surrogate. Alongside them are lesser-known figures like Baruch, the overworked administrator wrestling with his purpose, and Asaph, the gospel artiste frustrated by his struggle for visibility—among others.

Reimagined in modern-day settings, these stories uncover raw moments of doubt, failure, and heartbreak, illustrating how God's plan often unfolds in unexpected ways to bring about the best outcomes.

At the heart of the book is the Proposed Stages of Discouragement, a practical framework that helps you identify where you are in your own journey. The model takes you from the clarity of Clear Expectation and the optimism of High Hope, through the challenges of Disappointment, and into the critical stage of Reassessment—were decisions either lead to resilience or deeper discouragement. With the addition of a Recovery phase, the book provides you with tools and strategies to reframe setbacks, adapt, and rebuild.

If you have ever felt unseen, unworthy, or stuck, Discouraged meets you right where you are, helping you see your own story reflected in their struggles and discover the same hope they found. Through these stories and the practical guidance woven throughout, you will learn how to embrace resilience, navigate life's challenges, and trust that even in the darkest moments, God is still at work— and your story is far from over.

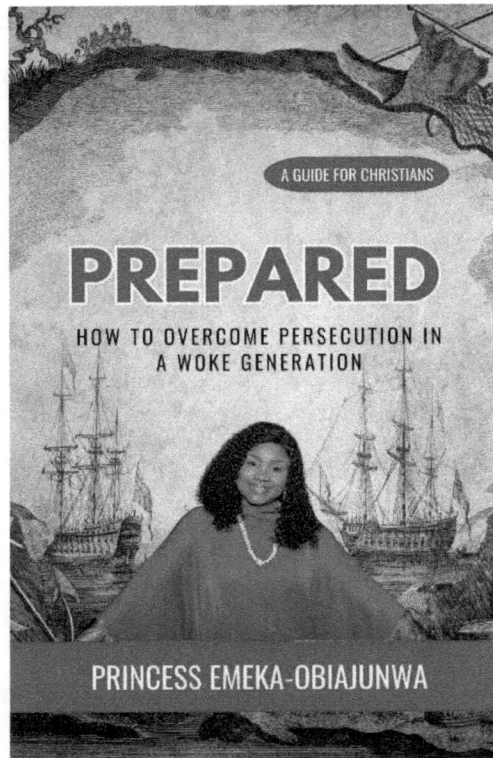

A GUIDE FOR CHRISTIANS

PREPARED

HOW TO OVERCOME PERSECUTION IN A WOKE GENERATION

PRINCESS EMEKA-OBIAJUNWA

Persecution has already begun—though not yet in its most violent form in some regions. Soon, believers will need extraordinary wisdom, wit, and courage to engage the world effectively while still shining their light. The test of our love will only intensify in the days ahead.

Are you prepared?

Prepared equips Christians to stand firm in their faith

while facing the challenges of persecution in a culture shaped by woke ideologies. This practical resource offers biblical guidance, real-world examples, and actionable strategies to remain steadfast amidst societal pressures and spiritual opposition.

From understanding the roots of woke culture to equipping the next generation with resilience and wisdom, prepared provides tools to help believers respond to cultural challenges without compromising their convictions. While it critically addresses woke ideologies, the book remains both accessible and Christ-centred for those grappling with these issues.

In prepared, you will find the insight and encouragement you need to handle difficult conversations, withstand persecution, and represent Christ in a world increasingly resistant to biblical truth.

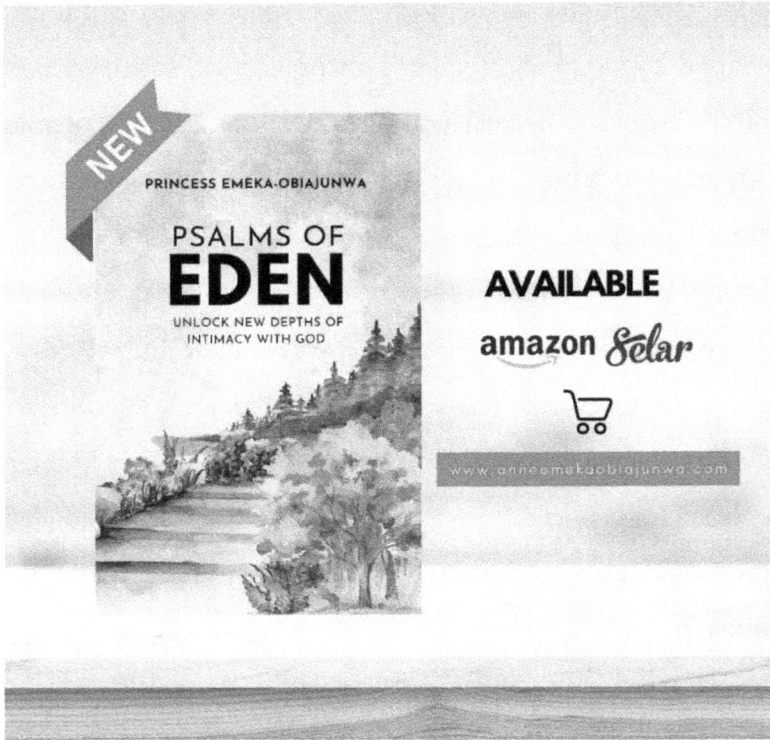

Psalms of Eden is a collection of heartfelt poems about loving the Lord. These words came from moments of worship, longing, surrender, and open conversations with God. Each poem is a doorway into exciting corners of Eden where new levels of intimacy will awaken within your spirit.

If you've ever wanted to express your love for God with more than words, these psalms will give voice to the parts of your heart that have always belonged to Him.

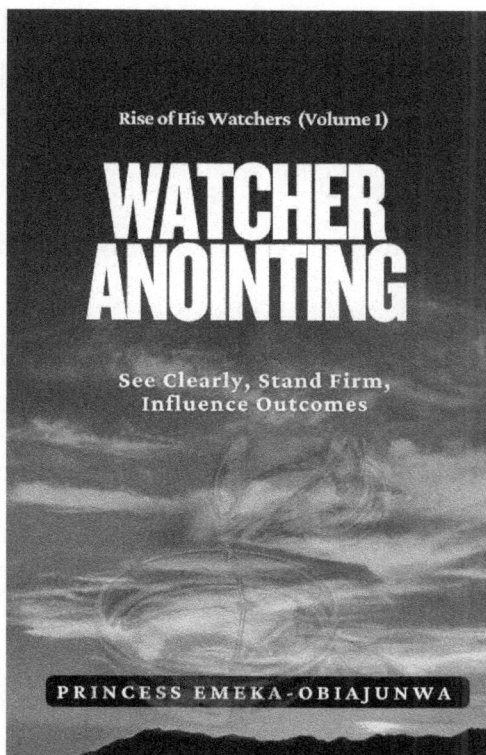

Rise of His Watchers: A Tetralogy

A calling like no other awaits those who are willing to rise. *Rise of His Watchers* is a four-part series that reveals the powerful, yet often misunderstood, role of the Watcher—believers chosen to partner with God in shaping lives, territories, and destinies. From seeing with clarity to governing with authority, this tetralogy equips you to step into a higher realm of influence and impact. Have you felt a stirring to carry God's heart for His people and to shape outcomes through prayer and decrees? **Watcher Anointing** reveals the unique identity, purpose, and skill set of spiritual Watchers—those called to stand as divine sentinels between heaven and earth. This book

- Provides practical insight into the role of a Watcher.
- Clears up misconceptions about the watcher ministry.
- Equips you to walk confidently in your calling.

You will

- Identify the Watcher call and anointing on your life.
- Discover the nine Watcher archetypes that help you find your unique place among watchers.
- Learn how to handle prophetic operations such as visions, trances, dreams, utterances, and words of

knowledge with wisdom and precision.

- Gain practical tools to influence your God-given sphere of assignment effectively.

If God has urged you into a higher place of intercession and spiritual authority, **Watcher Anointing** will give you the clarity and anointing you need to function as a watcher.

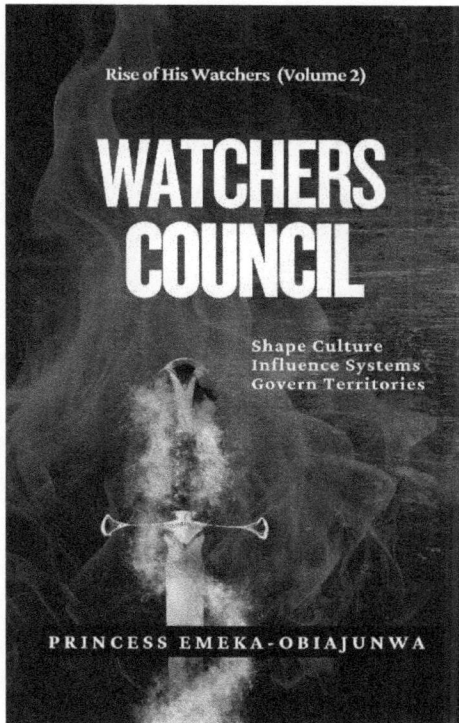

Rise of His Watchers (Volume 2)

WATCHERS COUNCIL

Shape Culture
Influence Systems
Govern Territories

PRINCESS EMEKA-OBIAJUNWA

Watchers Council unveils how spiritual decisions are

made and executed concerning families, nations, systems, and generations. It introduces you to the realm of Watcher angels; their assignments, jurisdictions, and how they partner with YOU. This book is for those who are ready to move beyond awareness into alignment with God's purposes in the places they have been called to stand. You will

- Discover the Book of Truth and how to engage it
- Understand the role and structure of the Watchers' Council
- Recognize the operations of Watcher angels over thrones, territories, and systems
- Discern spiritual tipping points for judgment, mercy, or restoration.
- Partner with Heaven to shape culture, influence systems, and govern territories.

HOW TO STAY ON
FIRE FOR GOD

PRACTICAL PRINCIPLES
FOR BUSY MOMS

PRINCESS EMEKA-OBIAJUNWA

Motherhood is a beautiful and demanding gift, but it can also become the place where a once vibrant daughter of God begins to lose her fire. What if you could stay on fire for God without adding more to your already full plate?

In *How to Stay on Fire for God*, Princess-Anne Emeka-Obiajunwa shares five fire extinguishers that every mother encounters and the key laws to keep your fire burning.

This easy and light-hearted read is filled with practical and relatable wisdom to help busy moms sustain their spiritual passion in the middle of everyday responsibilities.

As a special bonus, this book includes a 21-day devotional designed to help you rediscover intimacy with Jesus in a deeply personal way. Each day reveals a fresh aspect of Jesus, drawing you into a love-filled and life-giving relationship that will keep your fire burning for a lifetime. If you have been feeling dry, distracted, or distant from God, this book will help you reignite your fire and keep it burning.

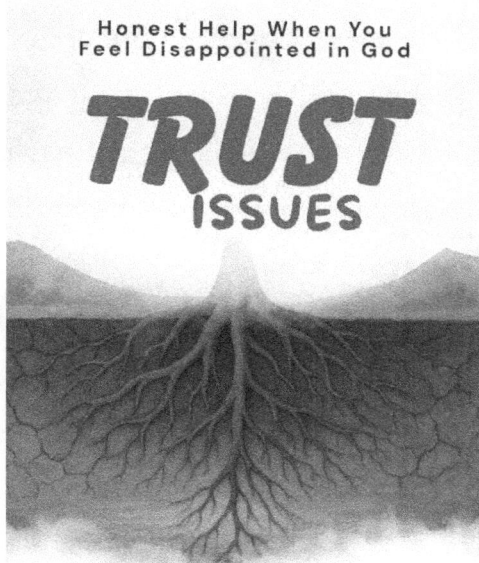

Honest Help When You
Feel Disappointed in God

TRUST ISSUES

PRINCESS EMEKA-OBIAJUNWA

Many believers are ashamed, afraid, or simply unwilling to admit they have felt disappointed in God at least once in their lives. Unacknowledged, that disappointment hardens into scar tissue that shapes what we dare to pray for and how high we are willing to jump when God says, "Jump!"

If you have tasted loss, grief, failure, or the long ache of unanswered prayer, this book is for you.

Drawing from her journey through repeated pregnancy losses and hard-won hope, **Princess** blends candid storytelling, Scripture, and research, from cognitive-dissonance studies to trauma-informed neuroscience and attachment theory, to illuminate the way back to trusting God.

Inside, you will learn to:

- **Map the drift** from first heartbreak to cautious faith and recognise where you are on that path.

- **Unmask the psychological, emotional, spiritual, and social "covers"** we wear to appear strong.

- **Identify six core emotions** that quietly fuel subtle distrust in God.

- **Give language to your ache** and follow a clear, step-by-step route toward wholehearted trust.

  Trust Issues offers no clichés. Instead, it provides research-rooted tools, biblical hope, and a lantern for the darkest stretches of the journey of life, so you can live like the tree in Jeremiah 17, unafraid when heat comes and fruitful in every season.

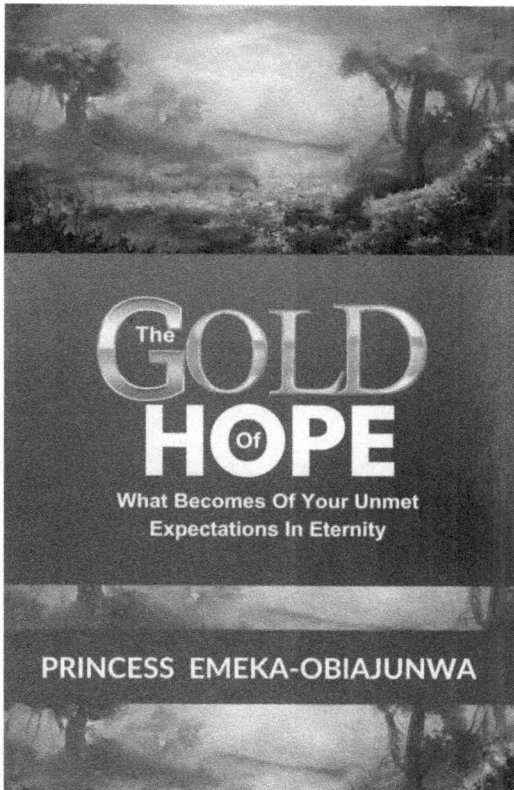

The gold of hope is a journey into the question every believer wrestles with but rarely voices: what happens to the prayers that go unanswered, the promises that seem forgotten, and the dreams that never come true?

The book speaks to the ache of unanswered prayers and the weight of expectations that never materialise, the healing prayed for that never came, the effort that still ended in failure, the miracle longed for that never arrived. On earth, these moments feel like disappointment. In heaven, they are shaped into something far more beautiful and enduring.

Drawing from lived stories and scripture, Princess-Anne Emeka- Obiajunwa's shares what becomes of our unmet expectations in eternity, just as the father graciously allowed her to see.

Apostle Paul saw it. King David knew it. Now, it is your turn to see it too!

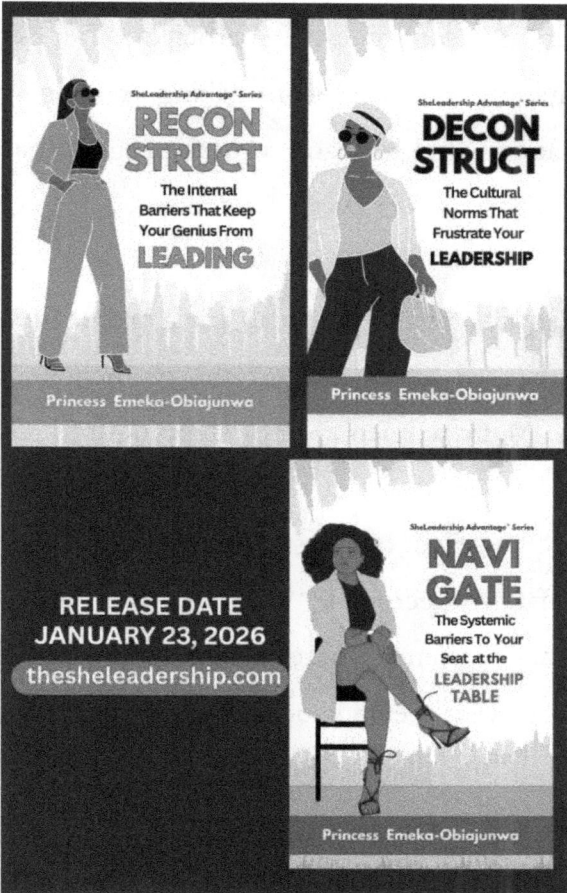

Women remain significantly underrepresented in leadership across every sector, even with global commitments such as the Sustainable Development Goals adopted in 2015. According to the 2024 Global Gender Gap Report, the world has closed only sixty-eight-point five percent of the gender gap. This means leadership, economic participation, political representation and decision-making remain unequal across nations, and in many regions progress has stalled or even reversed.

These statistics reveal the size of the gap, but they do not reveal the lived experience of the women behind the numbers. Many women are not stepping into leadership roles not because they lack skill, interest or aspiration, but because they face barriers that traditional leadership systems fail to recognize. These barriers are internal, cultural and systemic forces shaping how women see themselves, what they pursue and which leadership doors open or close to them.

For some women, the greatest barrier is internal. This may look like self-doubt, hesitation, fear of being judged, the feeling of not being ready, the pressure to shrink or the belief that leadership belongs to "stronger" or "louder" women. These internal messages accumulate over years of conditioning and convince a capable woman that she is not ready or not interested in leading. For others, the barrier is cultural. Cultural scripts shape how a woman sees herself, what she believes she is allowed to do and how much authority she can carry. Family expectations, faith, gender norms, community rules and inherited traditions, all influence how far a woman feels she is permitted to go. These cultural boundaries frustrate her leadership moves before she even gets a chance.

For many women, the barrier is systemic. Systems determine access, visibility, opportunity, sponsorship and advancement. Women often carry the weight of childcare, unpaid domestic responsibilities and emotional labor while pursuing study or building a career. Long hour cultures and institutional gatekeeping create a leadership pipeline that makes it harder for women to be seen, supported and advanced. Over time, these patterns can make leadership feel distant or costly, not because she is unable to lead, but because she is moving through structures that were not built with her in mind. When a woman faces any of these internal, cultural or systemic barriers, she can easily conclude that leadership is not for her, even when she is the next best thing to happen to an organization.

If leadership has ever felt distant, complicated or out of reach, the SheLeadership Advantage™ Series helps you understand why and equips you with the tools to:

RECONSTRUCT

The internal barriers that keep your genius from leading

DECONSTRUCT

The cultural norms that frustrate your leadership

NAVIGATE

The systemic barriers to your seat at the leadership table

Your sector does not just need more women. It needs you, your clarity, your perspective and your genius capacity to propel transformation. Whilst courage matters, courage on its own will not secure a seat at the leadership table. Many women are courageous yet still held back. What has been missing is a practical strategy for rising through the barriers that shape women's leadership journeys. The SheLeadership Advantage Series gives you that strategy.